Through the Thirds

A Systematic Approach to Planning Your Football Season

Tony Mee

DARK RIVER

Published in 2020 by Dark River, an imprint of Bennion Kearny Limited.

Copyright © Dark River

Tony Mee has asserted his right under the Copyright Designs and Patents Act 1988 to be identified as the author of this work

ISBN: 978-1-911121-88-6

All Rights Reserved. No part of this publication may be reproduced, stored in a retrieval system, or transmitted in any form or by any means, electronic, mechanical, photocopying, recording or otherwise, without the prior permission of the publisher.

This book is sold subject to the condition that it shall not, by way of trade or otherwise, be lent, re-sold, hired out or otherwise circulated without the publisher's prior consent in any form of binding or cover other than that it which it is published and without a similar condition including this condition being imposed on the subsequent purchaser.

Dark River has endeavoured to provide trademark information about all the companies and products mentioned in this book by the appropriate use of capitals. However, Dark River cannot guarantee the accuracy of this information.

Published by Dark River, an imprint of Bennion Kearny Limited
6 Woodside, Churnet View Road, Oakamoor, ST10 3AE

Acknowledgements

The knowledge that my grandchildren will not have to worry about inheriting Huntington's disease is a huge relief so, Austin, Holly, and Zack – this is for you – in the hope that others will be spared by my efforts to produce this book.

To my wife, Sally, and my daughters Lisa and Kelly, for their unwavering support for everything I've ever done. And to my parents Pauline and Dennis, for ensuring I always had a ball at my feet when I was a kid.

To every coach and player that I've ever had the pleasure to work with down the years, your thirst for knowledge and improvement has inspired me to learn more and think more about "The Beautiful Game".

To James Lumsden-Cook and his team at Bennion Kearny for backing this project without hesitation and also for their generous support for the Huntington's Disease Association.

To Magnus Olford, Lee Merricks, and the team at SportSessionPlanner.com for giving me early access to the new platform to create the diagrams.

To Doncaster Rovers FC for allowing me to work flexibly to develop young players around the demands of looking after my wife.

Finally, to Huntington's Warriors wherever you are in the world. At times it can feel like nobody outside your circle knows what you are going through; rest assured that you are not alone and, hopefully, there is a breakthrough around the corner.

Table of Contents

Preface	1
Introduction	3
Chapter 1: Formations and the players' roles and responsibilities within them	5
Chapter 2: Warm-Ups	31
Chapter 3: Pre-Season	43
Chapter 4: Developing Play from the Defensive Third	57
Chapter 5: Defending in the Attacking Third (High Press)	73
Chapter 6: Counter-Attacking (Regains in the Attacking Third)	91
Chapter 7: Developing Play Through the Middle Third (Creating the Attack)	107
Chapter 8: Defending in the Middle Third (Medium Block)	123
Chapter 9: Counter-Attacking (Transitions from the Middle Third)	141
Chapter 10: Developing Play in the Attacking Third (Finishing the Attack)	157
Chapter 11: Defending in the Defensive Third (Low Block)	171
Chapter 12: Transitions from the Defending Third	187
Conclusion	205

Preface

In 2013, my wife, Sally, was diagnosed with Huntington's disease.

Huntington's disease is a condition that stops parts of the brain working properly over time. It is passed on (inherited) from a person's parents. It gets gradually worse over time and is usually fatal. The symptoms typically start at 30 to 50 years of age, but can begin much earlier or later.

Symptoms of Huntington's disease can include:

- Difficulty concentrating and memory lapses
- Depression
- Stumbling and clumsiness
- Involuntary jerking or fidgety movements of the limbs and body
- Mood swings and personality changes
- Problems swallowing, speaking, and breathing
- Difficulty moving

Full-time nursing care is needed in the latter stages of the condition. As mentioned above, it is usually terminal; normally, about 15 to 20 years after symptoms start.

As my wife has unfailingly supported me – both as a player, and during my coaching career, I decided to give this book a go.

This book brings together over 30 years of coaching experience, 20 of which have been spent working in youth development with professional football clubs, to offer you – the football coach – a consolidated series of sessions to use with your players.

By sharing this experience, I hope to raise as much money as I can for the Huntington's Disease Association, who do so much good work for people suffering from this horrible illness, and who work tirelessly to help find a cure.

Thank you for your support. It is most appreciated.

Introduction

Everything starts with the ball and finishes with the ball. Sometimes we forget that this is a game with 11 v 11, WITH ONE BALL, and we try to keep this ball, we try to play with the ball, we try to make everything with the ball. **Pep Guardiola**

Well, if you're going to write a coaching book in the 21st century, you might as well start with a quote from the greatest coach of the current era (some will argue of all time, but history has a habit of proving people wrong).

I can't remember there ever being a time when I didn't have a ball at my feet. As a youngster, I'd be sent to the shop to buy my parents cigarettes (you could do that back then!), and I would take a ball, playing one-twos off the kerb, and scoring in the gaps between lamp post and wall – all the time running a commentary in my head. At school, we would play in the playground at every opportunity, and weekends would be filled with school games or pick-up games. If there were enough kids on our street, we would form our own team and play against other streets in the village, on any bit of grass we could find.

I watched the club that I currently work for, in the dark old days of the early 70s, from the crumbling terraces of the old Belle Vue ground. We would sit on the wall behind the goals to watch our heroes and then, at half-time, walk around and do the same behind the other goal. Or stand at the top of the Rossington End, behind the goal, and watch the light aircraft landing on the old Doncaster Airport during the game's quieter moments!

Later, as a soldier, I would consider it an honour to be selected to play for various Regiments and Corps with people from all over the country whose accents could be indecipherable, but who all shared one thing…

A DEEP LOVE FOR THE GAME OF FOOTBALL!

I became a coach whilst serving, first with the Royal Corps of Signals and then the Army Physical Training Corps. My selection for the latter was one of the proudest days of my life.

I did bits of coaching within my various teams and was also selected to become a part-time tutor for the Football Association, thanks to some superb mentoring from Joe Roach, then the Army's Director of Football and, at the time of writing, the Academy Manager at AFC Bournemouth. This encouraged me to start thinking a bit more about the game and also about the supplementary areas around it. The fitness side was an easy one, given my background, but I knew little of psychology, leadership, or strategic planning, so I started to read and try to broaden my horizons. Football coaching was a bit hit and miss back then, and there was very little in the way of coaching manuals, CPD events, or much else.

Then came the internet and things began to change. All of a sudden, there was access to a wider range of materials, ideas which people were happy to share, and clips of teams that we had only heard of (or watched play) once a year if they qualified for the European Cup or big International competitions. And all this led me to where I am now.

Having left the Army in 2002, after a 23-year career, I landed a job I could never have dreamed of when growing up in a South Yorkshire pit village. I secured a coaching job in the Centre of Excellence at Rotherham United and, due to a partnership agreement with a local 6th form college, a full-time role running the College Academy football team. All of a sudden, I was a professional football coach!

I began sharing my session plans via the new medium of social media and also began collecting everything I could that I thought might help me on my coaching journey. It was whilst sharing some sessions, recently, that I decided to put something together that would maybe benefit other coaches but, more importantly, raise some funds for an organisation which is very close to my heart.

Developing a Curriculum

Whilst it is true that anyone can throw a ball to a group of players and a game of football will break out, there is a lot more to coaching than that. I believe that it is important to have at least a basic plan of what you are going to coach, and when you are going to coach it.

The curriculum that I currently work from is based around a repeating, 12-week cycle. This gives us the opportunity to visit all areas of the pitch – both offensively and defensively – and work on attacking, defending, and transitions in equal measure. At our club, every fourth week is a consolidation week, where the coaches will revisit any area that they feel needs additional work.

This book will attempt to give you the tools to do something similar, regardless of the level that you are operating at. The practices are designed for the 11-a-side game and for different formations. They have all been delivered by Academy coaches, with Academy players, but I believe that anyone with a basic understanding of the game, and the ability to adapt to their numbers/formation/ability level, should be able to put a curriculum together that ultimately benefits not just their team, but the individuals that make up that team.

Session Structure

How you put your sessions together will depend on a number of factors – your experience, time available, numbers available, space available, etc. I work on a basic 5 step model that has worked for me over the years and reflects, I believe, a logical series of progressions.

1. Warm-Up
2. Technical work – passing drill or rondo type practice
3. Some form of opposed practice – functional practice or phase of play
4. Small-sided game (we rarely have the luxury of 11v11 at training)
5. Cool Down

Whilst some prefer the Whole-Part-Whole method (Play-Practice-Play, in the USA), I find that the steps above work well, and that players are regularly put into match-type situations which require them to come up with solutions which they will need during the matches that they play on the weekend.

Notes: Throughout the book, I have used male pronouns. This is purely down to the fact that I have worked, almost exclusively, with male footballers.

Where timings have been included, these are generally how long I have spent on a particular activity. You may need less, or more, time depending on how quickly your players pick up on each particular topic.

1
Formations and the players' roles and responsibilities within them

> " *I believe in work, in connections between the players, I think what makes football great is that it is a team sport. You can win in different ways, by being more of a team, or by having better individual players. It is the team ethic that interests me, always.* "
>
> **Arsene Wenger**

When I read coaching forums, one of the most frequently asked questions is, "What formation should I play"? The answer, I believe, is the one that gets the most out of the group of players that you have at your disposal. It's really a question that only the coach of that particular team can answer, and just requires a little thought.

The coach probably knows the answer already but is seeking validation.

- "I have two speedy wide players who have great energy" – play with wingers or wing-backs.
- "I have three players who all like to play centre-back, are good headers and comfortable on the ball" – play with a back 3!

In my opinion, once the first ball has been kicked, ALL formations need to have a degree of fluidity because the nature of the game is one of constant movement and interaction. In this chapter, I will show you some of the more popular formations currently used, and what I believe are the main roles and responsibilities in each position. These are the main three or four things that players need to be aware of within the game. There are, of course, many variables, but we should try to avoid information overload, and not clutter any player's mind excessively.

Chapter 1

There will be many other formations, but I will stick to the main ones that I have used as part of a club curriculum; they give players a broad knowledge base to work from. There are some similarities… after all, the role of the goalkeeper is, primarily, to keep the ball out of your goal! However, as we all know, there is much more to it than that, particularly as the keeper now uses his or her feet up to seven times more than they use their hands.

Every formation will have its strengths and weaknesses, and it will be the coach's job to find ways to both maximise and exploit them, depending on the game situation and your game plan.

So, the following formations, and the roles and responsibilities therein, are my take on the subject. They been used (and developed) within the professional club environment since 2002, with varying degrees of success. Remember – our role is to give the PLAYER every opportunity to develop within a TEAM environment, so choose your formation with this in mind, and ensure a positive experience for all.

The majority of coaches will discuss formations without including the Number 1. I prefer to use the maxim "A part OF the team, not APART from the team"; therefore, I include the goalkeeper in the following formations.

As the roles and responsibilities of the goalkeeper are a constant, however, I will outline that position just the once and not in each formation that follows. Given the evolution of the modern goalkeeper, we include them in many passing drills and rondos in order to help improve their footwork and ability on the ball.

Formations and the players' roles and responsibilities within them

Goalkeeper (All Formations)

In Possession

- Distribute early with accurate kicks, throws, and rolls.
- Support defenders when they have the ball, and be prepared to receive on either foot.
- Communicate with outfield players. Early decisions and clear, purposeful instructions.

Out of Possession

- Starting position relative to the position of the ball, and in line with the ball.
- Sweeper/keeper when the defence pushes up.
- Shot stopping – ready position, decision whether to catch/parry or punch. React to second chances.

Chapter 1

1-4-3-3

Full-Backs (1-4-3-3)

In Possession

- Try to get on the ball from the Goalkeeper.
- Recognise when to get forward to support the attacking play, and when to stay back.
- Look for forward passes which break lines.
- Recognise when to come inside with the ball, or when to receive it.

Out of Possession

- Try to be close enough to the opposition wide player to pressure their first touch.
- Try to show opponents inside until level with the penalty box, then show down the line.
- Look to take quick throw-ins on your side of the pitch.

Formations and the players' roles and responsibilities within them

Centre-Backs (1-4-3-3)

In Possession

- Be prepared to receive the ball from the goalkeeper.
- Try to play angled passes behind the opposition. Play sharp, quick passes to full-backs and midfield players.
- Attack aerial balls with power, purpose, and timing.

Out of Possession

- Recognise when to follow opponents short, and when to hold your position.
- Be comfortable playing 1v1 and 2v2, practice marking goal-side and ball-side.
- When full-backs show wide, move deep and centrally to defend crosses.

Chapter 1

Defensive Midfielder | CDM (1-4-3-3)

In Possession

- Try to release wide midfield players with passes which break lines.
- Try to get on the ball from the goalkeeper and defenders. Play forward quickly when possible.
- Encourage attacking midfielders to support when playing into forwards.

Out of Possession

- Drop in as a supplementary centre-back if the regular centre-backs are pulled wide.
- Provide a defensive screen, block passes into the strikers' feet or steal from the front.
- Be close enough to defenders to pick up second balls.

Formations and the players' roles and responsibilities within them

Attacking Midfielders (1-4-3-3)

In Possession

- Try to play quick combinations in midfield.
- Link play from back to front, and support forwards quickly. Recognise when to support beyond the strikers.
- Try to slide passes between the defenders to create chances.

Out of Possession

- Play a high-pressure game in midfield. Try to intercept passes.
- Break up the opposition play.
- Try to force the opposition to play wide or backwards.

Chapter 1

Centre-Forward (1-4-3-3)

In Possession

- Recognise when to shoot with power and precision.
- Show for passes into feet. Receive on the half-turn, if possible.
- When play is developing in wide areas, find space between defenders to attack crosses.

Out of Possession

- Try to make opposition play predictable.
- Force the centre-back to play risky passes.
- Try to prevent the ball going into midfield and win the ball from the "wrong side". (By "wrong side", I am referring to where the midfield player is already applying pressure and the attacking player applies pressure from the opposite side whilst recovering towards their goal.)

Formations and the players' roles and responsibilities within them

Wide Forwards (1-4-3-3)

In Possession

- Play high against the opposition full-backs, and threaten the space behind.
- Provide accurate crosses when high up the pitch.
- Work across the forward line to support the centre-forward and disrupt the defensive line.
- Recognise when to dribble or play quick combinations.

Out of Possession

- Provide defensive cover in wide areas; pin the full-back back.
- Stop opposition crosses.
- Track wide players.

Chapter 1

1-3-5-2

Centre-Backs (1-3-5-2)

In Possession

- Be prepared to take possession from the goalkeeper or other defenders.
- Try to play angled passes behind the opposition. Play sharp, quick passes to Wing Backs and midfield players.
- Be prepared to step out from defence with the ball if there is space to do so.

Out of Possession

- Be prepared to defend in 1v1 situations, delaying the attack when possible.
- Attack aerial balls with power, purpose, and timing.
- Develop a good understanding with your partners and communicate effectively.
- Try not to get drawn into wide areas.

Formations and the players' roles and responsibilities within them

Wing Backs (1-3-5-2)

In Possession

- Try to give width and depth to the attack when playing out from the back.
- Try to provide crosses from different angles in the attacking half of the pitch.
- Try to play angled passes behind the opposition or into the forwards' feet in the attacking third.
- Be prepared to play 1v1 in possession of the ball.

Out of Possession

- Recover to a defensive position quickly, to make a midfield five or a back five depending on where the ball is.
- Provide defensive cover in wide areas.
- Defend the far post area when the opposition is crossing from the opposite flank.

Chapter 1

Defensive Midfielder | CDM (1-3-5-2)

In Possession

- Try to release other midfield players and forwards with passes which break the opposition's lines.
- Be prepared to get on the ball from defenders and your goalkeeper.
- Communicate effectively with your teammates.
- Encourage attacking midfielders to support the attack when playing in the final third.

Out of Possession

- Provide a defensive screen, block passes into the strikers, and try to steal from the "wrong side".
- Drop in as a supplementary centre-back if they are pulled wide (vulnerable area in this formation).
- Be close enough to defenders to pick up second balls from tackles/blocked shots etc.

Formations and the players' roles and responsibilities within them

Attacking Midfielders (1-3-5-2)

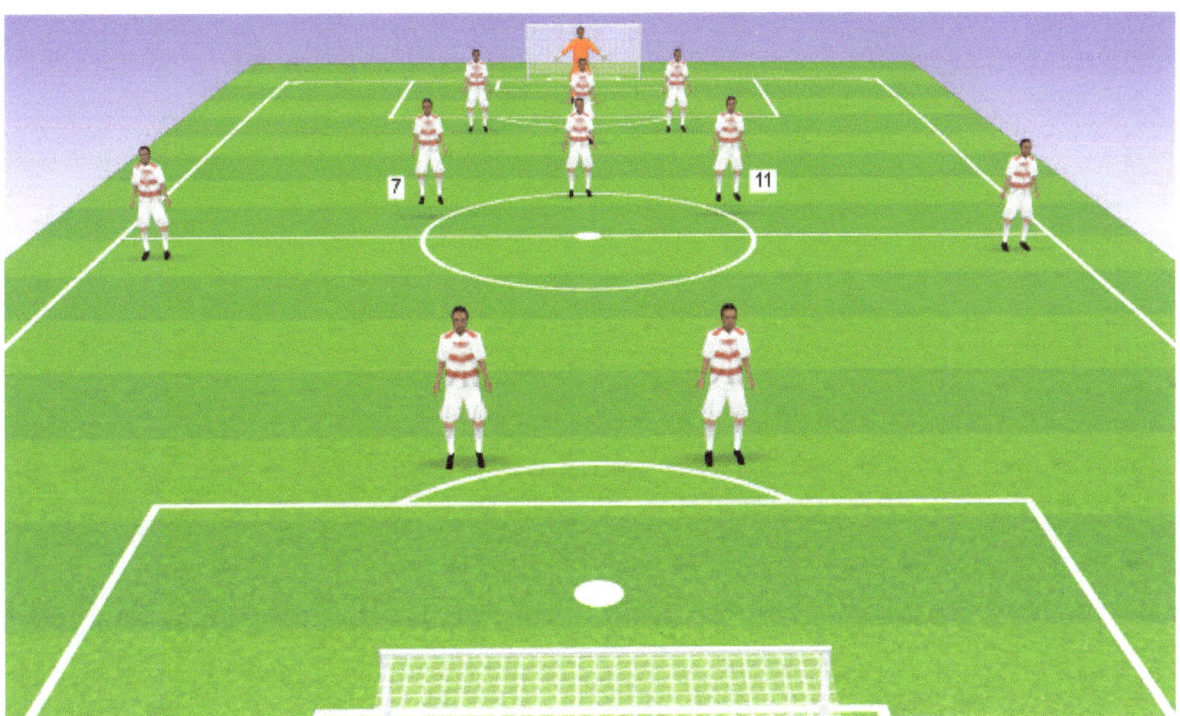

In Possession

- Try to play quick combinations – to shift the opposition – in the middle and attacking thirds of the pitch.
- Try to link play from, and to, the Wing Backs and forwards.
- Recognise when to run beyond the forwards.

Out of Possession

- Try to pressure your opponents quickly; try to intercept passes.
- Disrupt the opposition's build-up play.
- Try to force the opposition to play into congested areas, or backwards.

Chapter 1

Forwards (1-3-5-2)

In Possession

- Be positive and direct in advanced areas of the pitch. Shoot with precision.
- Show for passes into feet, and try to receive on the half-turn.
- When play is developing in wide areas, look for spaces between defenders to attack crosses.

Out of Possession

- Be an effective first line of defence.
- Force opposition defenders to play into central areas or make risky passes.
- Try to prevent the ball going into midfield and win the ball from the "wrong side".

Formations and the players' roles and responsibilities within them

1-4-2-3-1

Full-Backs (1-4-2-3-1)

In Possession

- Move high and wide to receive the ball from the goalkeeper when playing out from the back.
- Use a range of passes to help retain possession (into midfield players or forwards or switch play via defenders).
- Recognise opportunities to get forward as the ball travels towards your side of the pitch.
- Provide crosses to the forwards from advanced positions.

Out of Possession

- Be close enough to the opposition wide player to pressure his first touch.
- Recognise where to show your opponent (inside/outside) in relation to your cover.
- Try to seize the initiative in 1v1 duels.

Chapter 1

Centre-Backs (1-4-2-3-1)

In Possession

- Split wide and be prepared to receive the ball from the goalkeeper.
- Try to play angled passes behind the opposition to full-backs and midfield players, but recognise the need to play longer at times.
- Attack aerial balls with power, purpose, and timing.

Out of Possession

- Recognise when to follow opponents short, and when to pass them on.
- Be comfortable defending 1v1 and 2v2 situations; try to seize the initiative.
- Mark ball-side and goal-side.
- Recognise when to move deep and centrally in order to defend crosses.

Formations and the players' roles and responsibilities within them

Defensive Midfielders (1-4-2-3-1)

In Possession

- Drop into the space created by the centre-backs splitting, to give the goalkeeper options to play out from the back.
- Try to receive the ball sideways on, to play forward passes which break lines.
- Display a good range of passing; be prepared to initiate switches of play to exploit space in wide areas.

Out of Possession

- Be prepared to give cover to the full-back on your side of the pitch when he joins in the attack.
- Provide an additional defensive line and screen passes into the opposition forwards.
- Block shots, tackle, and spoil the opposition's game in midfield areas, and particularly at the top of the box.

Chapter 1

Wide Midfielders (1-4-2-3-1)

In Possession

- Try to be positive in 1v1 situations, particularly in the attacking third.
- Be prepared to support 9 and 10 in the channels (shaded), giving space to the full-back on the outside.
- Make penetrating passes into the forwards or overlapping full-backs, and crosses from wide areas.

Out of Possession

- Press or provide cover for the press high up the pitch. Win the ball back if you can (tackle or intercept).
- Provide defensive cover in wide areas, get on the outside of the holding midfield player (CDM). Double up against the opposition with the full-back.
- Track runners from deep or on switches of play.

Formations and the players' roles and responsibilities within them

Attacking Midfielder (1-4-2-3-1)

In Possession

- Try to play in-between the opposition's lines of defence (horizontally and vertically).
- Retain the ball and make positive runs and passes around, and in-between, the opposition's defence.
- Be prepared to shoot from distance, and support the 9 at all times.

Out of Possession

- Be prepared to press, or support the press, to make play predictable.
- If the opposition play with a playmaker, engage him high up the pitch to force longer clearances.
- Try to intercept or tackle in the midfield area to regain possession or make the opposition play backwards.

Chapter 1

Forward (1-4-2-3-1)

In Possession

- Recognise and take opportunities to shoot with power and precision.
- Be available to receive the ball into feet or space and on the half-turn if possible.
- Recognise when play is developing in wide areas and take up positions to attack crosses.

Out of Possession

- Initiate the team's press when appropriate.
- Try to force the centre-back to make risky passes.
- Try to prevent easy passes into midfield, and win the ball from the "wrong side" if midfield are holding play up.

Formations and the players' roles and responsibilities within them

1-4-4 (Diamond)-2

Full-Backs (1-4-4 (Diamond)-2)

In Possession

- Try to get on the ball from the goalkeeper.
- Recognise opportunities to go forward to support the attacking play in wide areas (shaded areas).
- Look for forward passes which break lines.
- Recognise when to come inside with, or to receive, the ball.

Out of Possession

- Recover to a defensive position quickly.
- Try to be close enough to the opposition wide player to pressure their first touch.
- Try to show opponents inside until level with the penalty box, then show down the line.
- Look to take quick throw-ins on your side of the pitch.

Chapter 1

Centre-Backs (1-4-4 (Diamond)-2)

In Possession

- Be prepared to receive the ball from the goalkeeper.
- Try to play angled passes behind the opposition.
- Play sharp, quick passes to full-backs and holding midfield player.
- Attack aerial balls with power, purpose, and timing.

Out of Possession

- Recognise when to follow opponents short, and when to hold your position.
- Be comfortable playing 1v1 and 2v2; practice marking goal-side and ball-side.
- When full-backs show opponents wide, move deep and centrally to defend crosses.

Defensive Midfield Player | CDM (1-4-4 (Diamond)-2)

In Possession

- Try to create space to receive the ball but be prepared to take it in tight situations.
- Try to receive the ball sideways on, allowing you to have the option to run, pass, or dribble forwards.
- Try to make passes which break lines to forwards or wide midfield players.

Out of Possession

- Provide cover for the back four (when full-backs go forward, be prepared to play in the space they leave).
- Screen the central defenders, preventing passes into the opposition forwards.
- Break up the opposition play.
- Try to force the opposition to play wide or backwards.

Chapter 1

Central Attacking Midfield Player | CAM (1-4-4 (Diamond)-2)

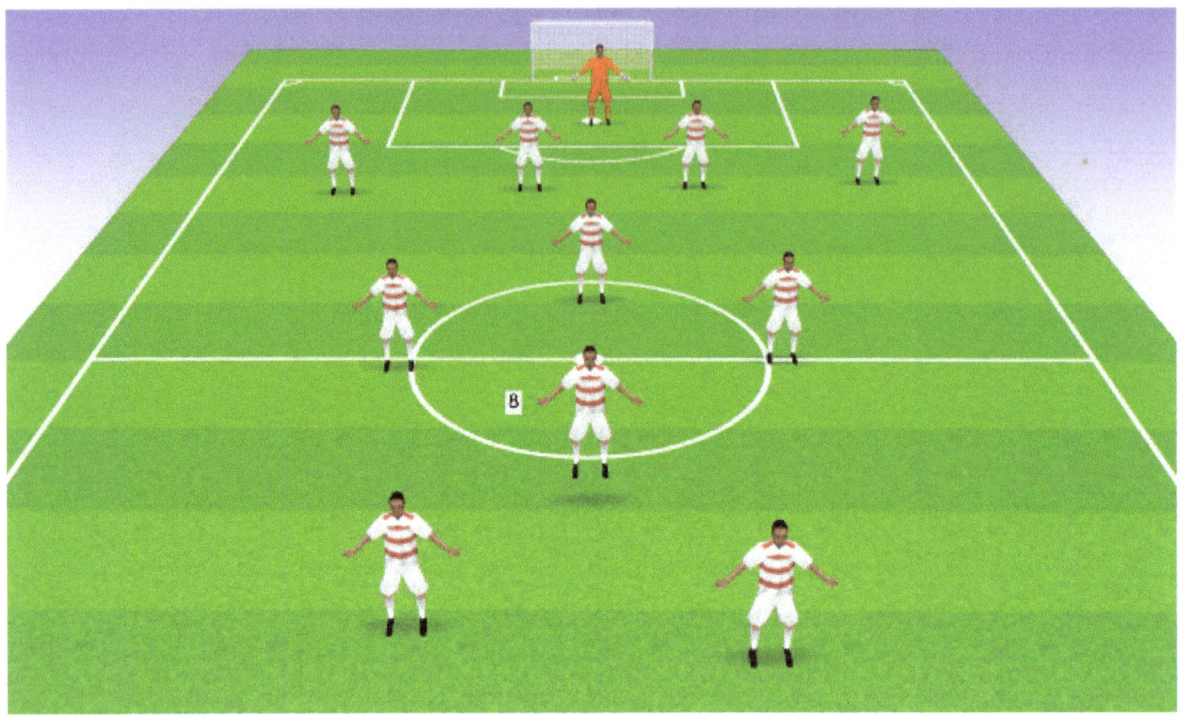

In Possession

- Try to create space to receive the ball but be prepared to take it in tight situations.
- Try to play in-between the opposition's defensive lines, and link play into the forwards and wide players.
- Try to support or play beyond the forwards when required.

Out of Possession

- Provide an additional line of defence when the front two are pressing.
- Break up the opposition play; try to win the ball from the "wrong side".
- Try to force the opposition to play wide or backwards.

Formations and the players' roles and responsibilities within them

Wide Midfield Players (1-4-4 (Diamond)-2)

In Possession

- Provide support to the attacks from the inside channels (shaded area).
- Combine with full-backs and holding midfield player to advance the ball up the pitch.
- Recognise when to dribble or play quick combinations.
- Try to be available to receive the ball at all times.

Out of Possession

- Make the central midfield area compact, and press to win the ball back.
- Provide defensive cover in wide areas.
- Close down shots and block forward passes in the defending third.

Chapter 1

Forwards (1-4-4 (Diamond)-2)

In Possession

- Recognise when to shoot with power and precision.
- Show for passes into feet, and receive on the half-turn.
- When play is developing in wide areas, find space between defenders to attack crosses.
- Recognise how to work as a pair (one up, one off - never on the same line).

Out of Possession

- Try to make play predictable. Try to prevent the ball being passed square across the back line.
- Force the centre-back to play risky passes.
- Try to prevent the ball going into midfield, and win the ball from the "wrong side".

2
Warm-Ups

> *Sometimes, a manager will assess the other team through the warm-up, and try to get an inkling as to what way they are going to be playing.*
>
> **John McGinn (Sheffield United)**

Warm-ups probably provoke as much debate as all other areas of the game combined. Many people will throw out such marvels as, "You don't see kids warming up before they go out to play".

Nonetheless, there are well-documented physical benefits to warming up, which include gradually increasing the heart rate and circulation, loosening the joints, and increasing blood flow to the muscles. Stretching the muscles prepares them for physical activity and helps to prevent injuries.

The warm-up is also a good opportunity for an individual to prepare themselves mentally for the game ahead, and for a team to work together prior to the start of the game. Warm-ups can also be used to practice skills and team drills. The warm-up should last as long as is required, but usually varies between 10 and 30 minutes. This could be dependent on a number of factors, including age group, time available, or even the prevailing weather conditions. However, I believe that some sort of preparatory work should be done before training and games.

I've seen a number of different methods carried out over the years: a video of Diego Maradona, laces untied, whistling along to the stadium music whilst juggling the ball; a Japanese team at a tournament in Spain performing a perfectly choreographed warm-up routine complete with chants and claps; and countless teams smashing balls around on local parks all over the country. Each coach will find a method that suits their purpose, but it is also important to recognise the needs of the individual, particularly as players get older. It is also important to try to allow time for some position-specific work during the warm-up, to help with the mental process and to help cement specific techniques.

Chapter 2

The warm-ups in this chapter are mainly ball-orientated and, when performed correctly, should help your players to be ready to go when the first whistle goes. I have included some passing drills in this chapter, which could also be used as an extension of the warm-up, but all coaches will have to develop an understanding of their players' and teams' needs.

Practice 1

FIFA 11 + Warm-Up

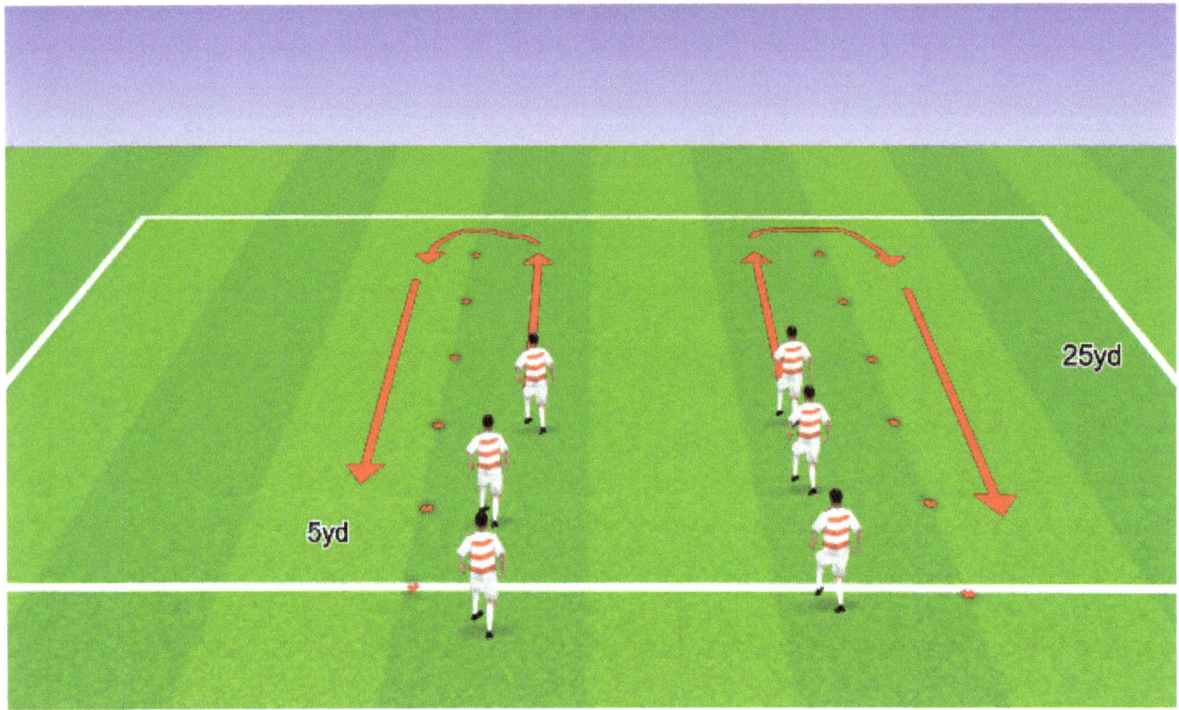

The course is made up of six pairs of parallel cones, approximately five-yards apart.

Two players start at the same time from the first pair of cones, jog along the inside of the cones, and do the various exercises on the way. After the last cone, they run back along the outside. On the way back, speed can be increased progressively as players warm-up.

Running Exercises (approx. 8 min)

1. Jog straight ahead to the last cone – two sets.
2. Jog to the first cone, lift knee to the front, then rotate outwards before lowering the leg (Hip Out). Jog to the next cone and repeat with the opposite leg – two sets.

Warm-Ups

3. Jog to the first cone, lift the knee to the side, then rotate to the front (Hip In). Jog to the next cone and repeat with the opposite leg – two sets.
4. Running Circling Partner – two sets (Jog to the first cone, shuffle sideways toward your partner, shuffle an entire circle around one another, and then shuffle back to the first cone).
5. Running Shoulder Contact – two sets (Jog to the first cone, shuffle sideways towards your partner – in the middle – jump sideways towards each other to make shoulder-to-shoulder contact. Land on both feet with your hips and knees bent).
6. Running Quickly Forwards and Backwards – two sets (Run quickly to the second cone, then run backwards to the first cone. Repeat, running two cones forwards and one cone backwards until you reach the end of the course).

Practice 2

Basic Passing and Movement Circle

Organisation

An equal number of players (if possible), working in pairs.

Chapter 2

An outside player starts with the ball and passes to a player in the middle. They manipulate the ball across the circle and pass to a different player on the outside, then go for a different ball.

Different dynamic stretches can be performed between changeovers.

Progression

Once the pass is made to the outside, the outside player dribbles in, and the inside player takes his place.

When the pass is received on the outside, the receiving player passes to another outside player before the ball is returned to the original player.

Practice 3

Advanced Passing Circle

Organisation

Players work in pairs for one minute then change roles (one serving, one working).

After performing the activity with the first server, players move on to a different server.

Warm-Ups

Various passes, body parts, controlling touches, etc.

- Ground passes – left foot, right foot.
- Half volleys – left foot, right foot.
- High Volleys – left foot, right foot.
- Chest control to volley (alternate feet from server to server).
- Standing header (low serve).
- Jumping header (high serve).
- **The coach should insist on good technique at all times.**

Full Pre-Match Warm-Up

Phase 1

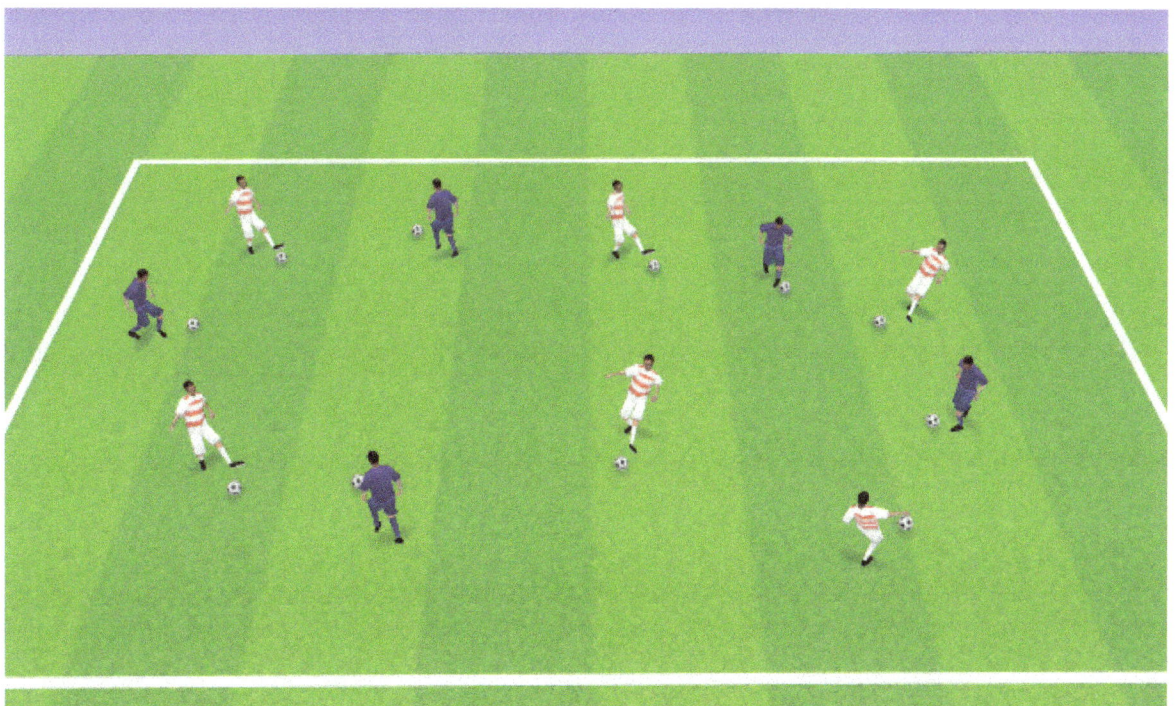

Organisation

Use the area in the corner of the pitch, between the touchline and the 18-yard box line (or a 20x20 yard box).

All players start with a ball and dribble around the area doing stops and turns, etc.

Dynamic flexibility at the player's discretion (players will have their own needs – particularly as they get older).

Chapter 2

Progression

Take away half the balls and now introduce passing and receiving.

Reminders to players about making eye contact, touches into space, etc.

Phase 2

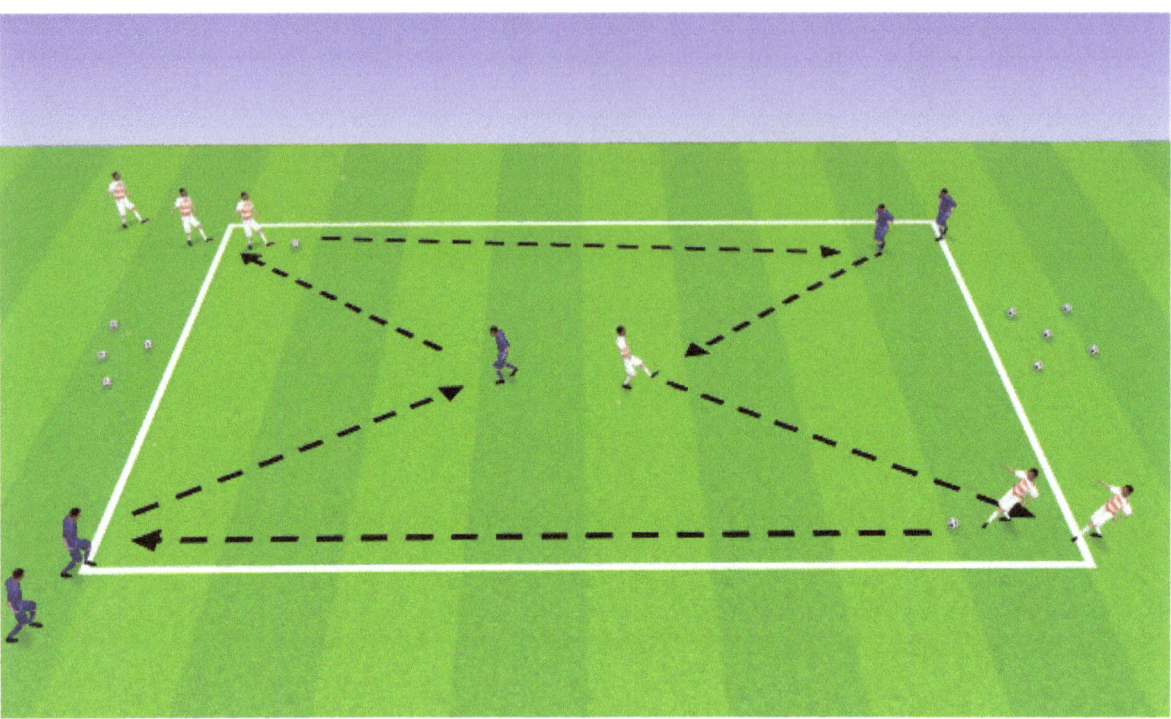

Organisation

Same area as before.

How to Play

Two balls at the same time starting from opposite corners.

Players pass and follow, in the direction of the arrows.

Once the pass has been made, players accelerate and decelerate.

Change direction and increase the pace of runs.

Phase 3

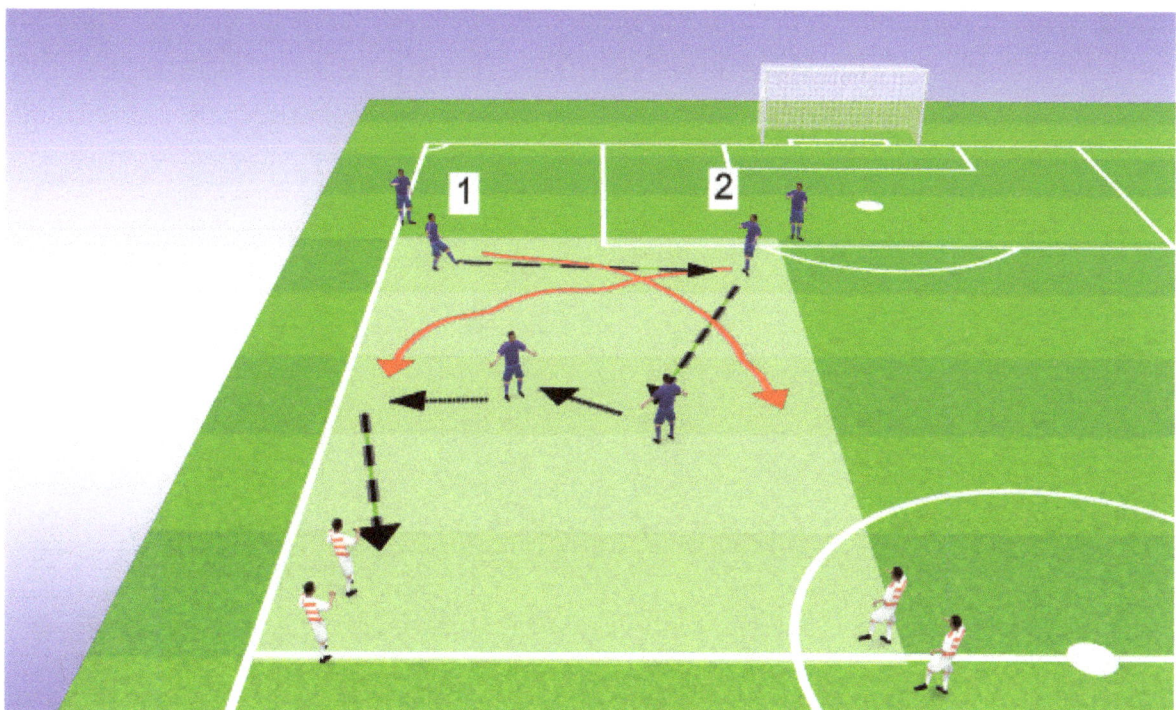

Organisation

Set up as shown with the two players in the middle – usually ones who play close to each other in the game (e.g., two strikers, two centre-midfielders, etc.)

How to Play

Start with a pass from player 1 to player 2.

Player 2 passes into the middle, and players 1 and 2 make the runs indicated by the curved arrows.

The two central players combine and pass to either of the runners.

Repeat from the opposite end.

Chapter 2

Phase 4

Organisation

Same area as the last practice. Play an SSG (Small-Sided Game); in this case "Line Ball" where teams score by taking the ball over the end line under control.

Phase 4 (alternative)

Same area with a coned square in the middle. One player from each team is in the square – try to pass to the middle player then take his place.

Passing Practices

Practice 1: Basic Passing Diamond

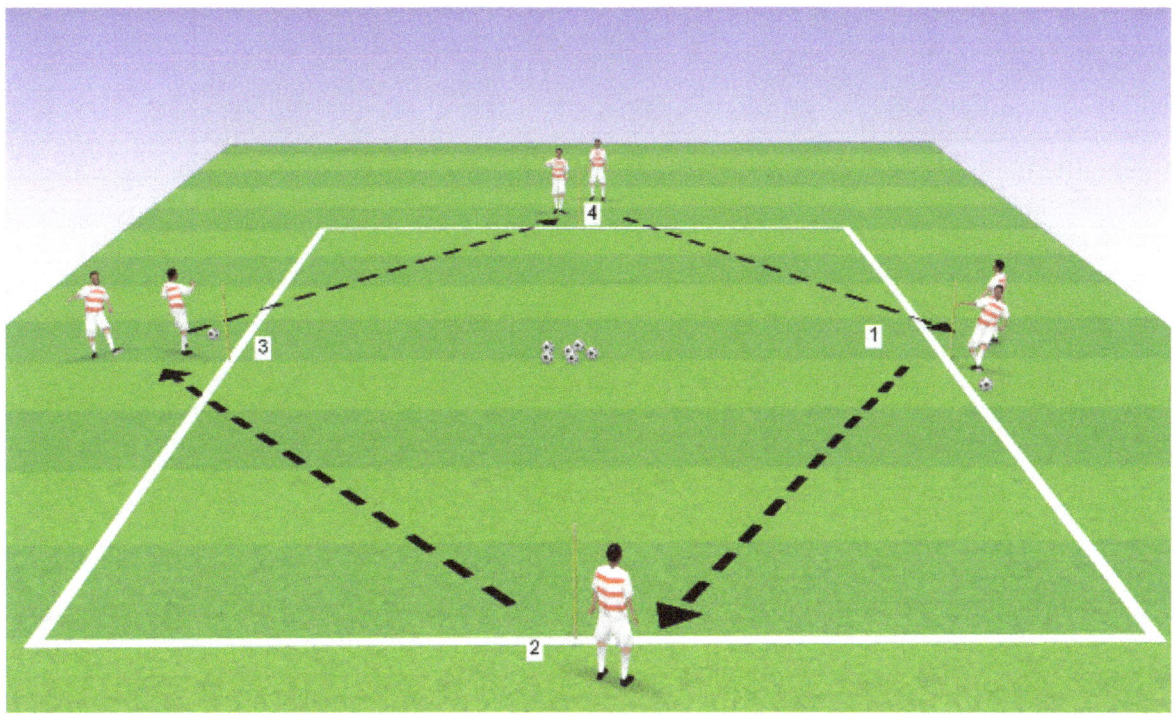

Organisation

Area size to suit the ability of your players.

Two balls in play.

How to Play

Pass and follow your pass to the next pole.

Receive on the back foot, and open up with your first touch to play the next pass.

Possible Coaching Points

- Accuracy and pace of the pass.
- Movement away from the pole to receive.
- Good first touch to change the angle of the ball.
- Try to play in one or two touches.

Progressions

Change direction.

Add a "set" and pass (1-2 around the pole) into the pattern.

Chapter 2

Practice 2: Modified Passing Diamond

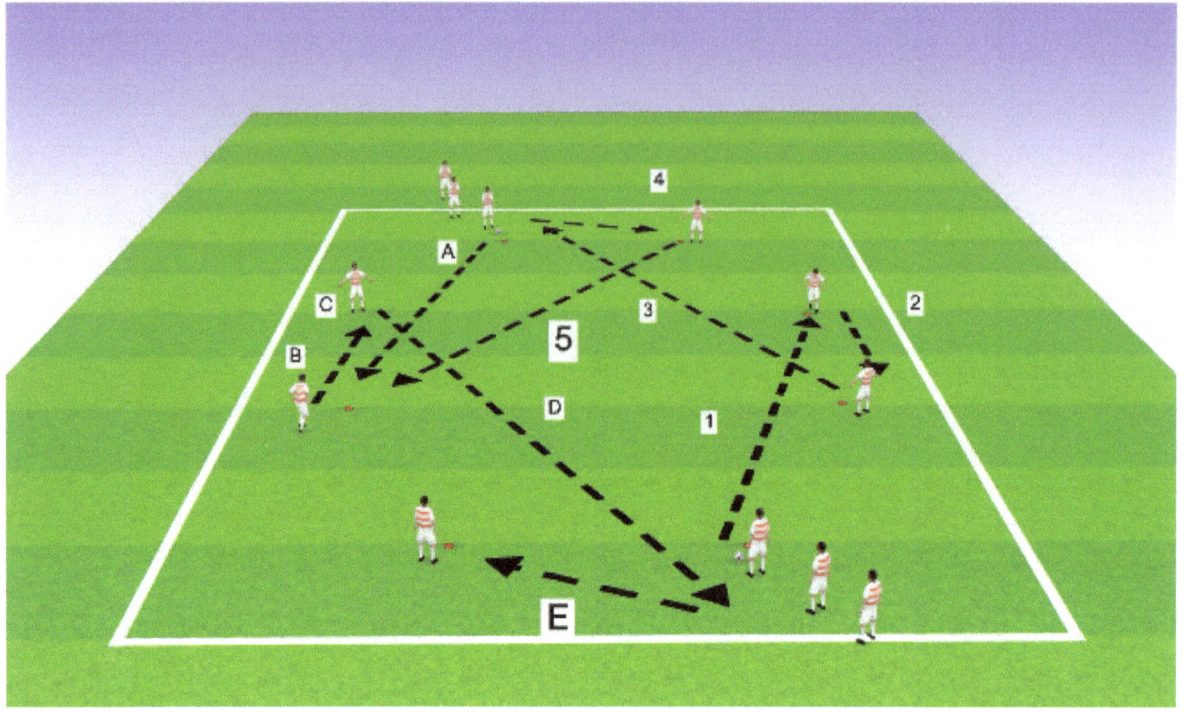

Organisation

The area can be manipulated to work on both short and long passing.

A larger area will give your players more thinking time.

Work for a set period of time in one direction then work in the opposite direction.

How to Play

A two ball exercise, with the balls starting in the position shown.

Passes are made in the order shown (on the left A-B-C-D-E, on the right 1-2-3-4-5).

The passer follows his pass and takes the place of the player at that disc.

Try to play in one or two touches.

Possible Coaching Points

- Pace and accuracy of the pass.
- Receiver to make a check movement and indicate where he wants the ball.
- On the short passes, try to leave the ball playable for the next player (don't pass a problem on to the next player).
- Follow the pass at pace.

Warm-Ups

Progression

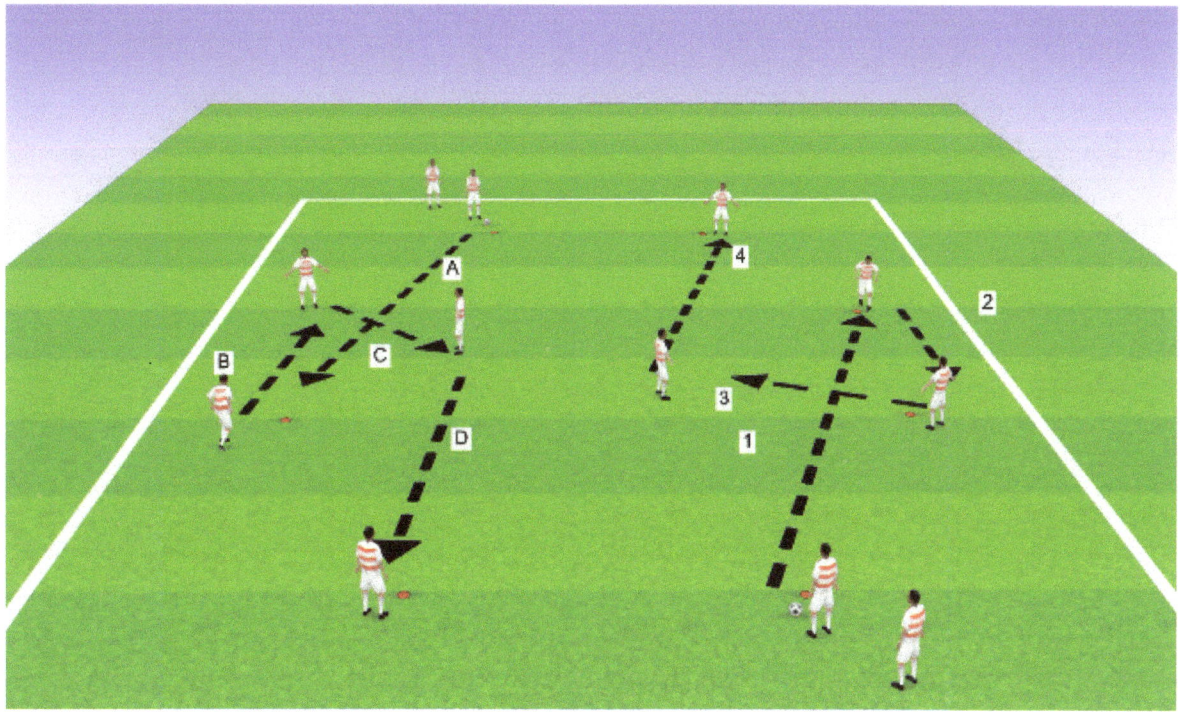

Add another player in the centre of the pitch on each side.

The practice then continues, as illustrated.

Practice 3: Passing and Movement

Chapter 2

Organisation

The area size is dependant on your numbers. Split the group into two teams. One team stand in the gates, one team with a ball each.

Perform each of the following for approximately one minute, then change over.

How to Play

Dribble and make 1-2 passes with the player in the gates.

Dribble and perform takes with the player in the gates. (A "take" is where the player in possession dribbles towards another player and, on a pre-determined call, the player without the ball takes it from the player with the ball).

Pass to the player in the gate and tell him to turn; the passing player takes his place in the gate.

Players have a choice of the above three practices.

Possible Coaching Points

- Dribbling technique.
- Passing and receiving.
- Playing with heads up (observation and scanning).
- Clear communication.
- Turning techniques.

3
Pre-Season

> "Pre-season isn't just about conditioning, but also getting used to each other as a team and a group of men. You spend more time with these people than you do your own family. Pre-season is the time we get used to each other, and work out how people work. It can be a lot of fun. Hard but fun."
>
> **Colin Kazim-Richards**

Many players dread pre-season as it can be a period of intensely gruelling training sessions, often two or three times per day, with the intention of getting all players as fit as possible for the upcoming season. Unfortunately, it can have the opposite effect, leaving players with sore muscles at best, or with severe injuries at worst. Hill runs, track sessions, and cross country runs have (and probably still can, with some thought) be used to try to get players ready for the competitive phase of the season. However, I will try to give you a number of different sessions that are ball-orientated, and which you can use to develop football-specific fitness alongside other exercises (depending on the age of the players that you are working with).

Fitness brings out the worst in some coaches, feeling that they have to be the Sergeant-Major figure on the side-lines, bawling at their players to perform various exercises and shuttle runs in order to develop their fitness. It is an industry in which many theories are espoused about when youngsters should be exposed to "exercise" – be that weights, aerobic training, anaerobic training, or developing strength and power. You can find many academic papers on the subject, and they will sometimes give opposing points of view. In general, the younger players are, the more under-developed their bodies, energy systems, and muscular systems are; in turn, the game of football itself is enough to develop fitness. Time spent with the ball is never time wasted, so try to spend as much time as possible with it.

Chapter 3

As players reach and go through puberty, coaches need to be aware of the effects on the young player, and training may need to be restricted during this period due to the increased risk of conditions such as Osgood–Schlatter and Sever's disease. Whilst there are many benefits to bodyweight exercises and weight training, it is important that correct form and technique are used and this is an area that coaches are probably not experts in. I see so many coaches giving players press-ups and sit-ups (often as punishment), but with no idea about how those exercises should be performed.

REMEMBER – work within your limitations. If you don't have the knowledge, find someone who does or concentrate on the reason that the players are with you – **TO PLAY FOOTBALL!**

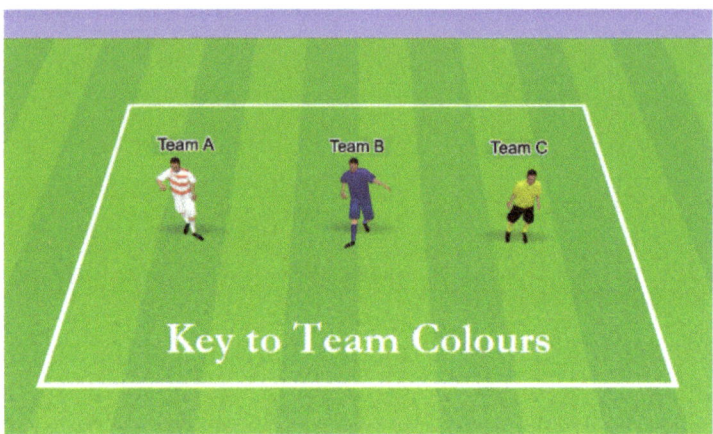

Pre-Season 1

Pass and Move

Pre-Season

Organisation

Adjacent areas 10x10m.

Three groups of players numbered 1-6.

How to Play

Players must pass in sequence.

Four minutes per round. One minute rest between rounds.

After a player has passed the ball, they leave the square via a pole and perform strides or dynamic stretches to another pole before rejoining the group.

Each round consists of the following:

1. Must have three touches before passing.
2. Must have two touches before passing.
3. Ball stays off the floor, three touches before passing.
4. Ball stays off the floor, two touches before passing.

Technical Work

Organisation

Players work in groups of three, around two mannequins or poles.

Chapter 3

Set up as many areas as required. One working, two serving.

One minute for each set of exercises.

How to Play

The player at the mannequin starts centrally each time:

1. Shuffle laterally to return passes: left foot, left side, right foot, right side.
2. Server throws the ball underarm for inside foot volleys: left and right.
3. Same service to thigh control and volley back with the opposite foot.
4. Throw service for chest control, volley back with laces.
5. Headers, left foot forward one side, right foot forward opposite side.

Switch to one ball per group.

1. Receive behind mannequin: first touch in front and diagonal pass to opposite server – back off behind mannequin and move laterally to repeat.
2. Underarm serve for diagonal volleys.
3. Underarm serve to bounce next to mannequin for diagonal half-volleys.
4. Underarm serve for chest control for diagonal side-volleys.
5. Underarm serve for diagonal headers.

SSG

Organisation

Goals positioned as shown. (If you only have two keepers, use back-to-back goals. If you have only one keeper, use a central goal but players can score from either side).

Two equal teams.

How to Play

Two teams compete to score in any of the three goals.

Time periods to suit your needs.

No stopping the game to coach (use water breaks).

If a goal is scored, but the ball stays in play, the game continues.

If GK makes a save, serve to an empty space.

Pre-Season 2

Technical Work

Chapter 3

Organisation

Players work in groups of three.

Areas to suit (10 yards long x 8 yards wide).

Ball at both ends.

One minute each.

How to Play

Players at the ends can serve anywhere in their box.

The player in the middle must cross the middle line each time.

1. Ground passes: left and right feet at both ends.
2. Volleys: left and right feet at both ends.
3. Thigh control to volley: right thigh to left foot and vice versa.
4. Chest to volley: left foot one end, right foot the other end.
5. Headers: standing header back to the server, run to server and touch the ball, back off to a jumping header.

Pass and Move

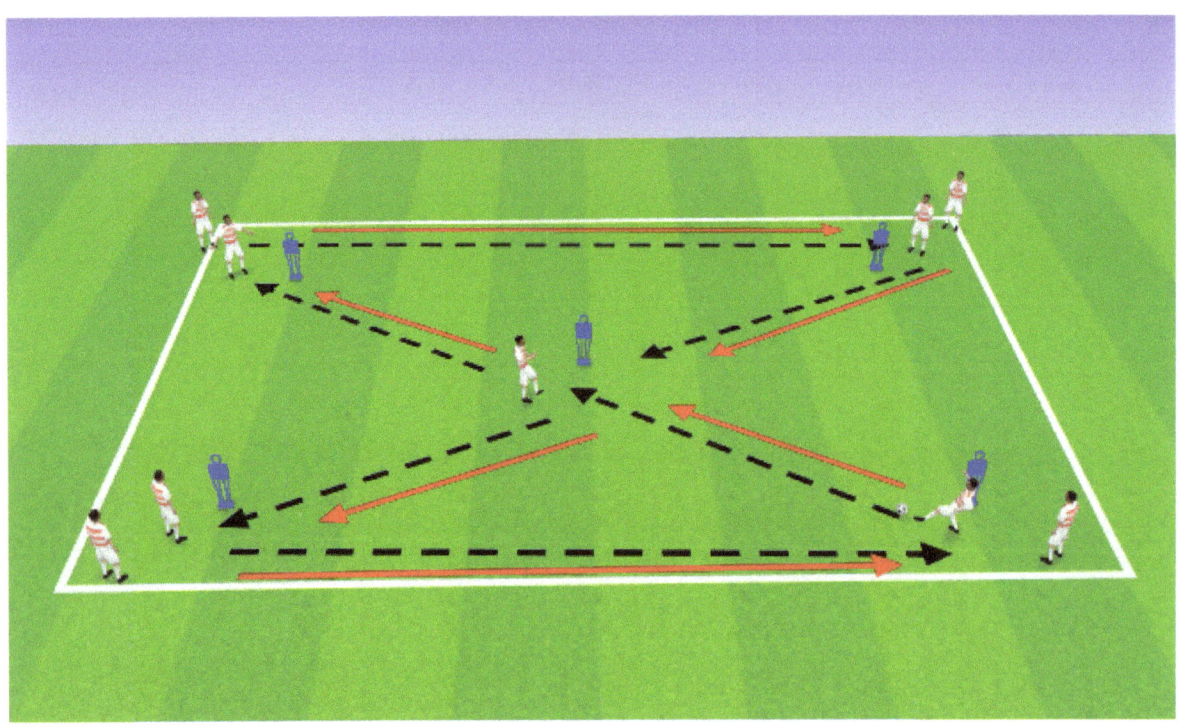

Pre-Season

Organisation

Mannequins are approximately 15 yards apart, with one placed in the middle.

Players are stationed as shown.

How to Play

Players pass in the direction indicated.

After the pass, players must **sprint** to the next position.

Technical Points

Receive on the back foot with hips "open".

Check away from the mannequin to receive.

Play off the second touch where possible.

Progression

Add a second ball from the opposite start position.

Pass and Move 2

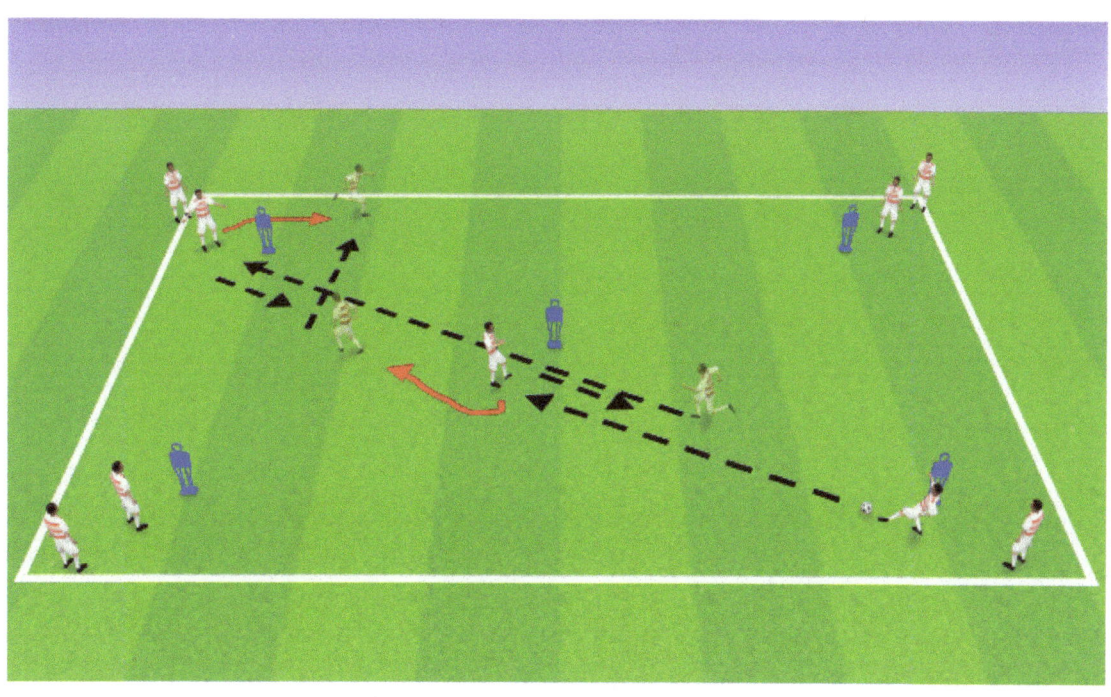

Chapter 3

Pass, set, and spin.

One-two in the corner.

Repeat from opposite corner.

SSG

Organisation

Pitch set up as shown, with a ball placed on top of each of the outer cones.

Equal numbered teams (if possible).

Two x 15 minutes.

How to Play

Normal game rules except:

1. If a player kicks the ball out, he must recover the ball from wherever it goes.
2. Meanwhile, the opposition can restart by taking any ball off any of the cones.
3. The player recovering the ball must replace it on the empty cone.
4. If a team scores, they keep the ball but restart from their keeper.
5. If the ball is deflected behind for a corner, the team in control keep possession from their own keeper and a defender has to recover the ball.

Pre-Season 3

Technical Practice

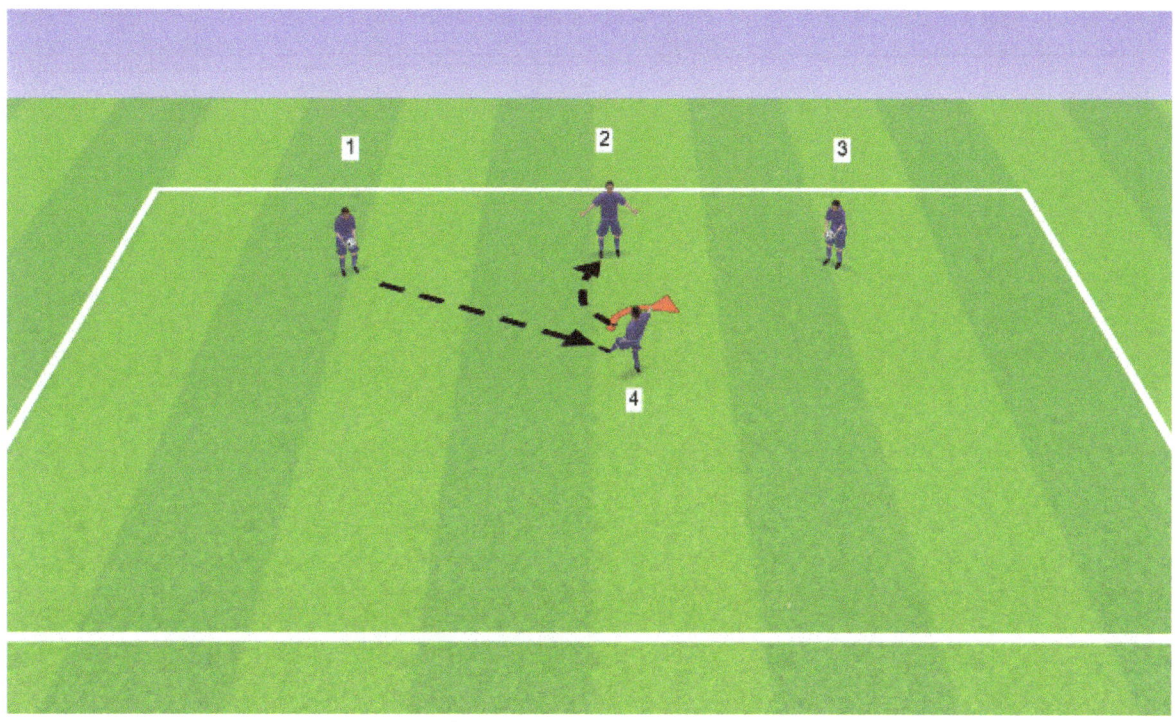

Organisation

Players in groups of four.

Area less than 10 yards square.

Players 1 to 3 (two players have a ball, and one does not) serve and receive. Player 4 works.

30-second rotations.

How to Play

Player 1 serves to Player 4 who passes to Player 2.

Player 3 serves and the pass goes to Player 1.

- Passes along the ground.
- Half-volleys.
- Volleys.
- Thigh to volley with opposite foot.

Chapter 3

- Chest volley.
- Headers.

The sequence continues with passes made to the player without a ball.

Pressing

Organisation

50 x 50 yards area.

Three equal teams.

Five-minute games.

How to Play

Two teams combine to keep possession from the third team (Teams A and B keep the ball from Team C).

The defending team press the ball and count all touches.

After all the teams have defended, the team with the fewest touches performs a forfeit.

Corners Game (30 mins)

Organisation

Pitch marked as shown.

Two teams with GKs.

How to Play

Both teams are instructed in style of play (POFTB > Playing Out From The Back).

Any ball going out of play results in a corner to the opposite team.

All outfield players have to get into, or around, the box; GKs must sprint to the halfway line.

Chapter 3

Pre-Season 4

Rondo (20 mins)

Organisation

25 x 25 yards.

8v4 possession.

Three x two-minute rounds; one minute rest – all in touches.

Three x two-minute rounds; one minute rest – three-touch max.

How to Play

The team of four count the number of touches they make.

The two lowest-scoring teams receive a forfeit.

Pre-Season

Anaerobic Practice (30 mins)

Organisation

Set up the pitch as shown.

How to Play

Player A plays to striker.

As soon as the pass is played, Team A's players support the attack and Team B's players recover to defend.

Team A try to score, Team B defend the goal.

Team C are resting.

As soon as the attack has ended, Team A become defenders (one player at the 18-yard line, and the others sprint back to halfway line); Team C become attackers, and Team B move to rest.

Each team has four attacks.

Progression

If the defending team wins the ball, they counter to the halfway line.

Chapter 3

SSG (20 mins)

Organisation

Pitch set up as shown.

Two x 10 minutes.

How to Play

Normal rules (no offsides).

All players must be in the attacking half for goals to count.

If a team scores, they restart the game from their goalkeeper.

If a team wins a corner, they restart from their goalkeeper.

4

Developing Play from the Defensive Third

> " Sometimes, people misunderstand when we talk about build-up that it always has to be short passes. If we want to play the ball into our front three from goal kicks, or into the space with a longer quality pass for them to receive in a 1v1, and it's on to do so, then we will take that. "
>
> **Kevin Betsey, England U15 Coach**

With all the subsequent sessions within this book, make sure that you give your players the opportunity to play in the positions that you expect them to play in during your games. Experience in other positions is invaluable, but the older players get, the closer they will be to playing in a set position (or a set area of the pitch at least).

Chapter 4

Practice 1

Organisation

Simulated Formations Throughout

Team B: 1-4-2-3-1

Team A: 1-3-5-2

Area is 30x30.

Team B consists of four defenders and two defensive midfield players.

Team A will be three forwards and three midfield players.

Each team has a target player on the end line (rotate periodically).

Both teams should try to play within their "lines" (mark with flat discs).

Two x 10 minutes.

How to Play

Team B start with the ball and try to play, through their forward players, to the target player on the end line.

Developing Play from the Defensive Third

If Team A recover the ball, they try to do the same.

Play always restarts with the team that reaches the target player getting a new ball from behind their end line.

Possible Coaching Points

- Quality of passing and receiving.
- Angles and distances of support.
- Creating and exploiting space.
- Recognising the forward passing opportunity.

Line Ball (25 mins)

Organisation

Increase the area size, as shown.

The 6-yard line and halfway line are now Target Lines (take the ball over, under control, to score).

How to Play

Team B starts in possession and try to score over Team A's 6-yard line.

Chapter 4

If Team A recover the ball, they try to score over the halfway line. If a team scores, they start from their backline.

Players can now move around the pitch more freely but MUST retain their basic formations.

Possible Coaching Points

- As per the previous practice.
- Black team rotation in outside areas (if left-back advances, the left sided centre-back can go to the touchline and one of the two central defensive midfield players drop in to fill the space).
- If the centre-back drives out with the ball, a central defensive midfield player drops in to cover.

SSG (25 mins)

Organisation

Half a pitch.

Introduce goalkeepers.

How to Play

Normal rules, including offsides.

Developing Play from the Defensive Third

Possible Coaching Points

- All from previous exercises.
- In all small-sided games, look for opportunities to practice the principles of play worked on during the session.

Practice 2

Three team rondo (25 mins)

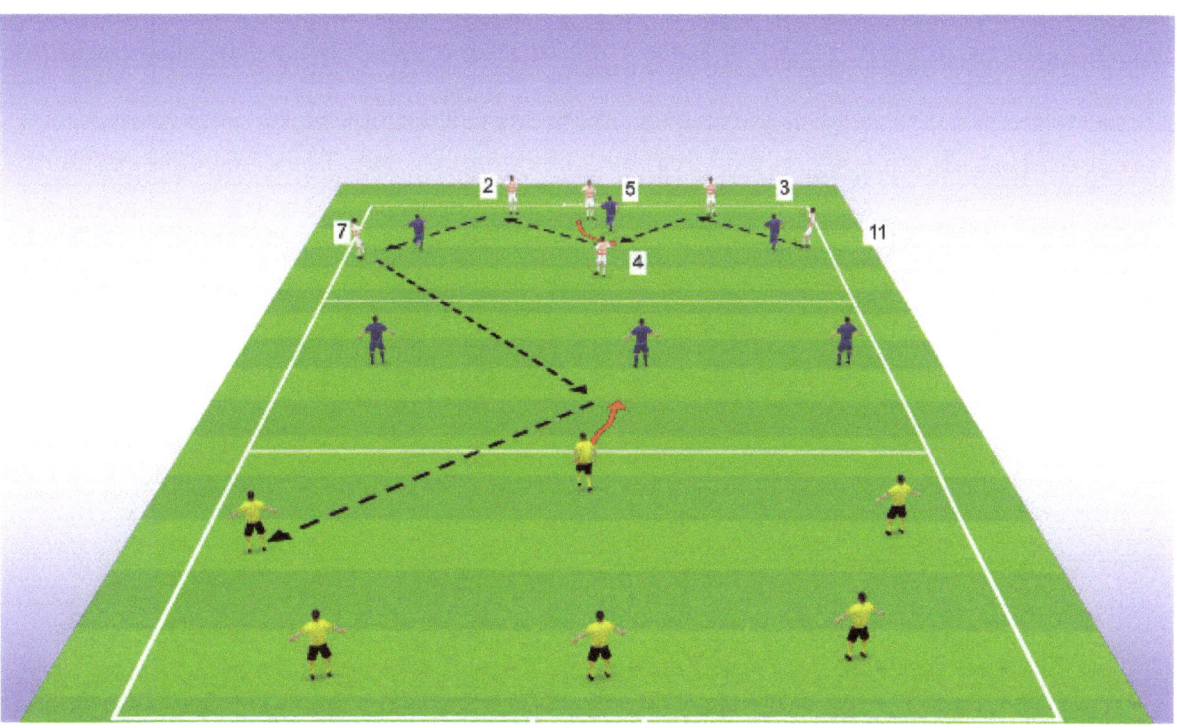

Organisation

Intervals:

Four-minute rounds; three minutes work + one minute of rest x six = 24 minutes.

Set up:

End zones are 35x20. Middle zone is 35x12.

Three equal teams where possible (six players each, in this example).

In possession, set up with a back three (numbers 2, 5 and 3) & three midfield players.

Chapter 4

Defending team presses with three players plus three in the middle zone.

How to Play

If Team B regain the ball, score one point for playing behind the centre-backs (setup 8-yard wide gate).

Must make a set number of passes in the zone before the option to transfer to the far zone.

Team C may send a player into the midfield zone to help transfer; or numbers 4, 7 or 11 can drive into middle zone and play forward.

Possible Coaching Points

- Number 4 plays high to give depth.
- Centre-backs stepping into the middle to provide more passing options.
- Finding the link player in middle zone or driving out with the ball (decision making).

8v6 build-out of back (25 mins)

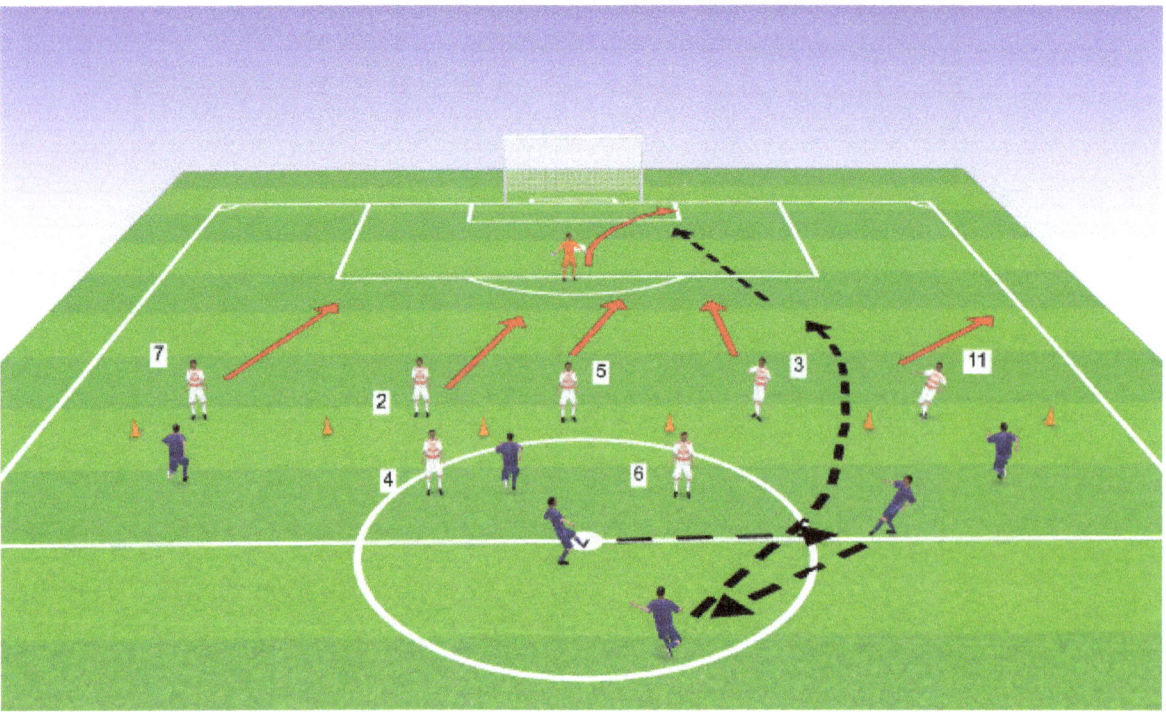

Organisation

Half pitch, set up as shown.

Developing Play from the Defensive Third

Defending team (Team A) in 1-5-2.

Attacking team play with six players and press high out of possession (three forwards, three midfielders).

Three target gates, as shown, for the defending team to score through when playing out.

How to Play

Team B's midfield play square passes to move the defence around. On the coach's whistle, play a long through-ball for forward runners.

Team A must defend and then build-out of the back through one of the three gates.

Team B is trying to score in the big goal.

Progression

Goal Kicks

Throw-ins

Possible Coaching Points

- Play simply, secure the ball, and play the way you face in transition to attack (this might mean playing backwards).
- Goalkeeper should create passing angles (usually outside of the goal).
- Goalkeeper should protect the space behind back three (start position), and then drop off to create more distance for a back pass.

Chapter 4

11v11 (30 mins)

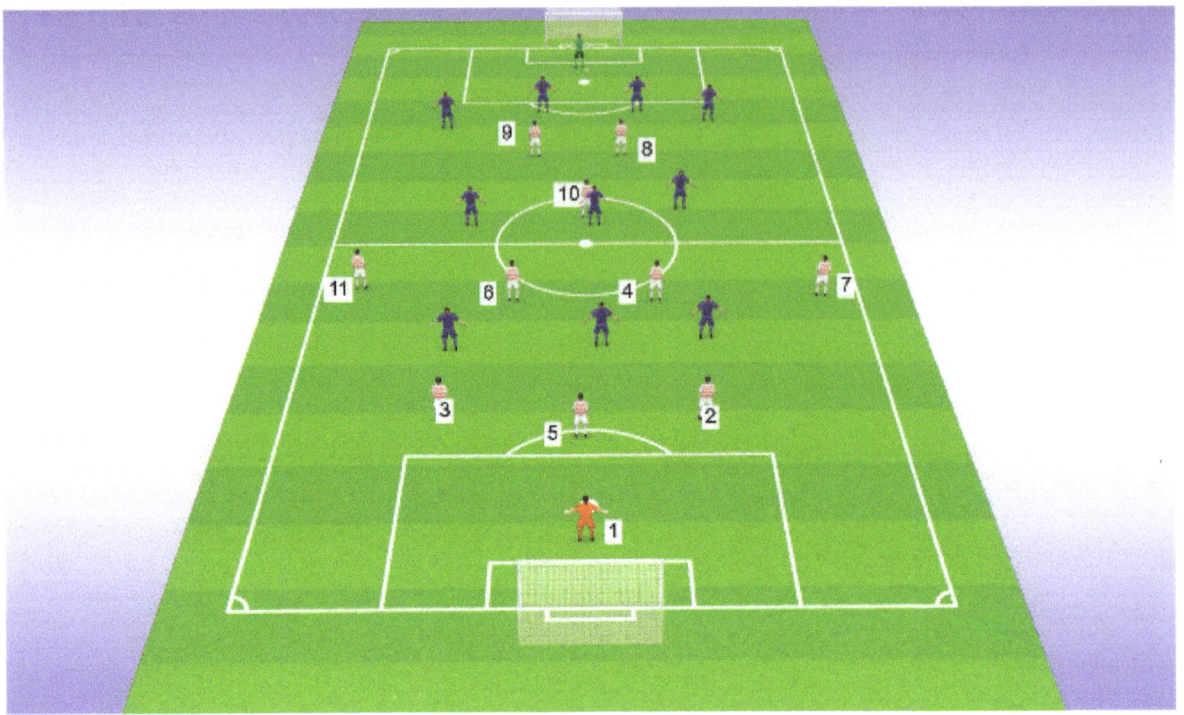

Organisation

Full pitch.

1 team in 1-4-3-3.

1 team in 1-3-4-1-2.

Could be done as a phase of play if you don't have 22 players.

How to Play

Normal rules.

Team playing 1-4-3-3 must complete 10 passes before scoring.

Possible Coaching Points:

- Centre-backs stay fairly narrow to avoid passes being played through.
- Angled passes to 4/6 and 7/11.
- Only one of 4/6 should drop deep.
- Pass or drive forward when you can.

Developing Play from the Defensive Third

Practice 3

Passing and Receiving (15 mins)

Organisation

Pitch set up as shown.

Team B in appropriate formation.

Team A in a loose 2-3-1, depending on numbers.

How to Play

Both teams start with a ball and pass through each other's lines to shoot at goal (Team A) or pass to the target (Team B).

Ensure Team B play to the principles of play. (Realistic passes, match tempo, appropriate connections/combinations).

Chapter 4

Functional Practice 1 (25 mins)

Organisation

Pitch set up as shown.

Teams organised in formation.

Team A can play anywhere on the pitch up to the outside lines.

How to Play

Play starts with Team B's goalkeeper and, to begin with, must go into the shaded zone.

Team B should retain shape at all times.

Try to work the ball, through good passing and movement combinations, into the number 8 and 9.

Developing Play from the Defensive Third

Functional Practice 2 (30 mins)

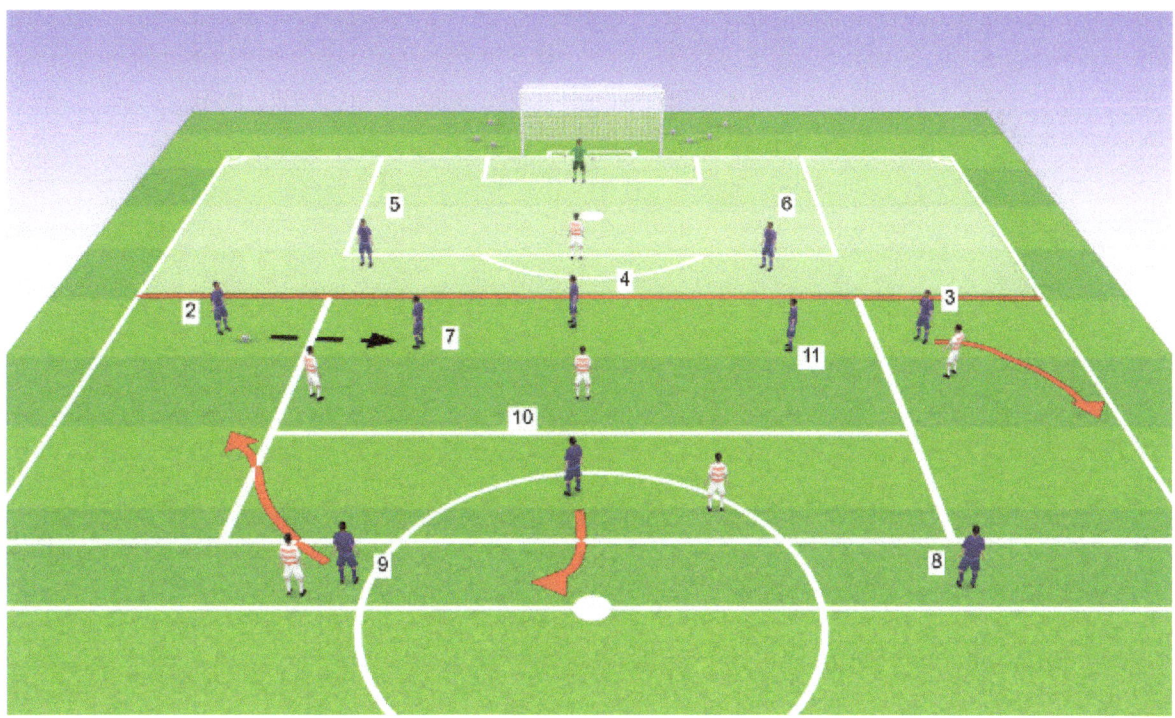

If a striker (8 or 9) drops short to receive the ball, the number 10 should move forward as shown by the hatched lines and arrows.

With play in the opposite channel with number 2, number 3 should move towards the middle of the pitch.

If the pass goes into the middle zone – to 7 or 4 – number 3 should move higher and wider.

Chapter 4

SSG (30 mins)

Organisation

Play on half a pitch.

If you only have one goalkeeper, use target areas (shown with poles) for the defending team to play out to.

Normal rules, use the 18-yard line as an offside line for the attacking team.

How to Play

Allow as much free play as possible to allow both teams to problem solve.

Coach what you see, if it is relevant to the earlier parts of the practice.

This includes the goalkeeper throwing or passing the ball into the midfield three, or the striker if he is left 1v1.

Practice 4

Functional Practice (25 mins)

Organisation

Half pitch with a target zone extending back 15 yards from the halfway line.

Team A play in formation (1-3-5-2 shown - no strikers or goalkeeper) defending a mini-goal.

Team B play 1-4-3-3 (no defenders or goalkeeper) in opposition, defending the target zone.

Supply of balls at each end.

How to Play

Initial play from Team A with Team B's attackers restricted to the 18-yard line.

On the second Team A player's touch, everyone goes "Live".

Team A try to advance the ball into the Target Zone, under control.

Team B try to stop them and score in the mini-goal from inside the 18-yard box.

Chapter 4

If Team A run the ball into the Target Zone, Team B can pick up one of the spare balls and start a counter-attack.

Possible Coaching Points

- Patience in possession – don't force play.
- Use the width of the pitch – switch play.
- Create and use overloads.
- Switch on to transitions.

FP2 (30 mins)

Organisation

As previous exercise, but with a goalkeeper and full-size goal behind Team A.

The spare goalkeeper plays as a target player in the target zone.

How to Play

As previous exercise, but Team A now have the option to play longer, into the Target player **BUT** the ball must reach him without bouncing.

Developing Play from the Defensive Third

SSG (30 mins)

Organisation

Half a pitch.

Two teams, even numbers with goalkeepers.

If your players aren't confident playing out, it may be worth starting with a "retreat line". (A retreat line is a pre-determined point which the opposition must stay behind until the team playing out cross it).

How to Play

One of the teams should start with your back three players.

Both teams play to the principles of your game.

Allow as much free play as possible to allow for decision making, but challenge teams to play out from the back.

5
Defending in the Attacking Third (High Press)

> " *If you watch me during the game, I celebrate when we press the ball and it goes out.* "
>
> **Jurgen Klopp**

With all the subsequent sessions within this book, make sure that you give your players the opportunity to play in the positions that you expect them to play in, during your games. Experience in other positions is invaluable, but the older players get, the closer they will be to playing in a set position (or a set area of the pitch at least).

Chapter 5

Practice 1

Pressing Practice (15 mins)

Rondo

Four teams of two players.

The team that loses possession defends.

Rules

Defenders stay in if:

- 10 consecutive passes
- Split pass
- Nutmeg

Possible Coaching Points

- Nearest player closes down the player in possession quickly.
- Supporting defender covers at an angle (try to make the next pass predictable).
- Good communication.

Defending in the Attacking Third (High Press)

Positional Game (20 mins)

Organisation

Create an area 45 x 15 yards, split into thirds with the middle third divided into two.

Use three teams with either a neutral player or coach to start the game.

How to Play

The team in possession have to complete four passes before they can attempt to transfer to the team in the opposite end third.

The team that is defending sends two players to try to win the ball back while the other two players can intercept any attempted transfers but must be in the same half at all times.

Whichever team loses possession then becomes the defending team.

Progression

Create a competition where the first team to transfer the ball five times is the winner.

Chapter 5

Possible Coaching Points

- Middle players – try to either press or drop off, depending on whether there is pressure on the ball or not.
- Pressing players – try to keep pressure on the ball to prevent a transfer or drop off to make the transfer difficult.

Phase of Play (20 mins)

Organisation

Pitch size to suit your players, with a retreat line (shaded area).

Team A - numbers 1, 2, 4, 5, 6, 8, 9 + two mannequins as numbers 7 & 11.

Team B - numbers 3, 4, 6, 8, 7, 11, 9.

Starting point with Team A who have eight seconds to score.

How to play

Team A - Combine to score by passing to a mannequin or by scoring in the goal (must be over the red line before shooting).

Defending in the Attacking Third (High Press)

Team B (coached) - Win the ball high up the field using a team press and try to score (there must always be at least one defender behind the red line).

Normal football rules apply except no corners.

Player Tasks

Number 9

- Pressure centre-back by closing down on his touch and forcing play in one direction.
- Prevent switch of play.

Numbers 7 & 11

- Pressure their full-back as quickly as possible, forcing play inside towards team-mates.
- Opposite winger to tuck in when the ball is on the opposite side.
- Track the full-back if he goes forward.

Numbers 6 & 8

- Pressure the player on the ball in midfield.
- Prevent their midfield getting on the ball facing forward (try to force play back to where it came from, STOP THE SWITCH).
- Can you intercept to keep possession?
- Screen/Prevent easy ball through to their striker.

Numbers 3 & 4

- One player pressures their striker when he has the ball, the other covers.
- Prevent the ball being played to their wingers (mannequins).

All players should make recovery runs if the ball breaks their defensive line.

Chapter 5

SSG (20 mins)

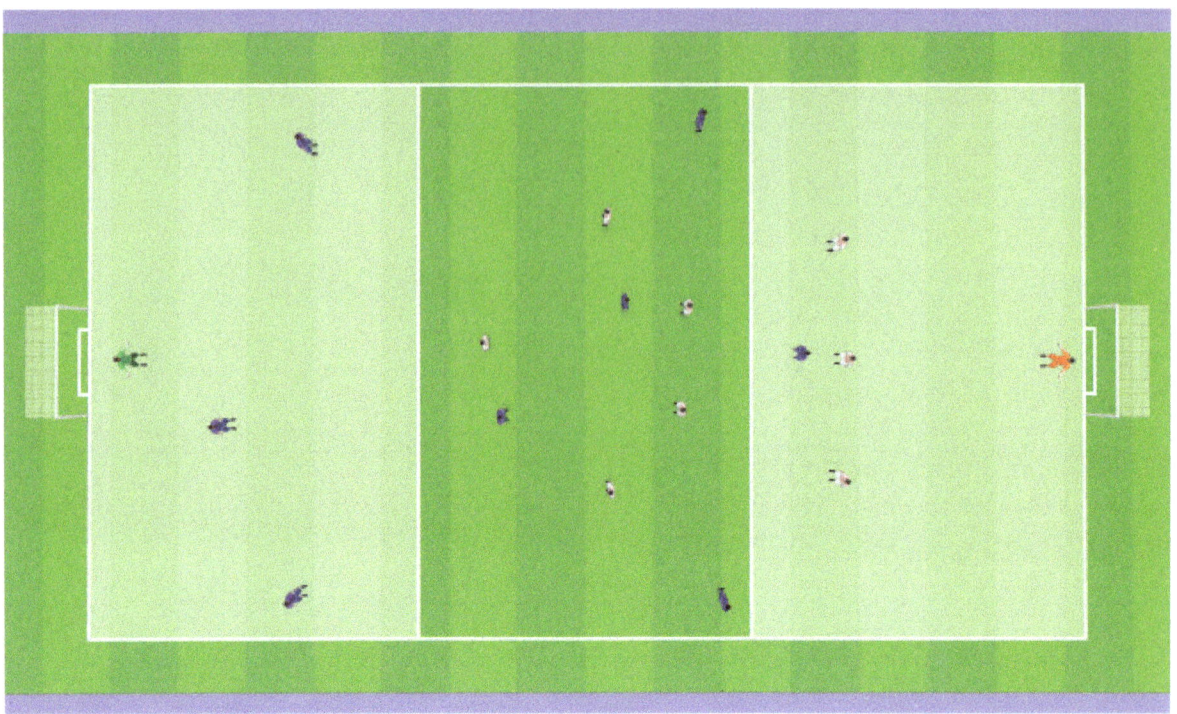

Set Up

9v9 pitch with retreat lines.

Normal football rules apply.

Strikers must drop behind the retreat line but can press on the outfield player's first touch.

Defending in the Attacking Third (High Press)

Practice 2

Press and Transition (20 mins)

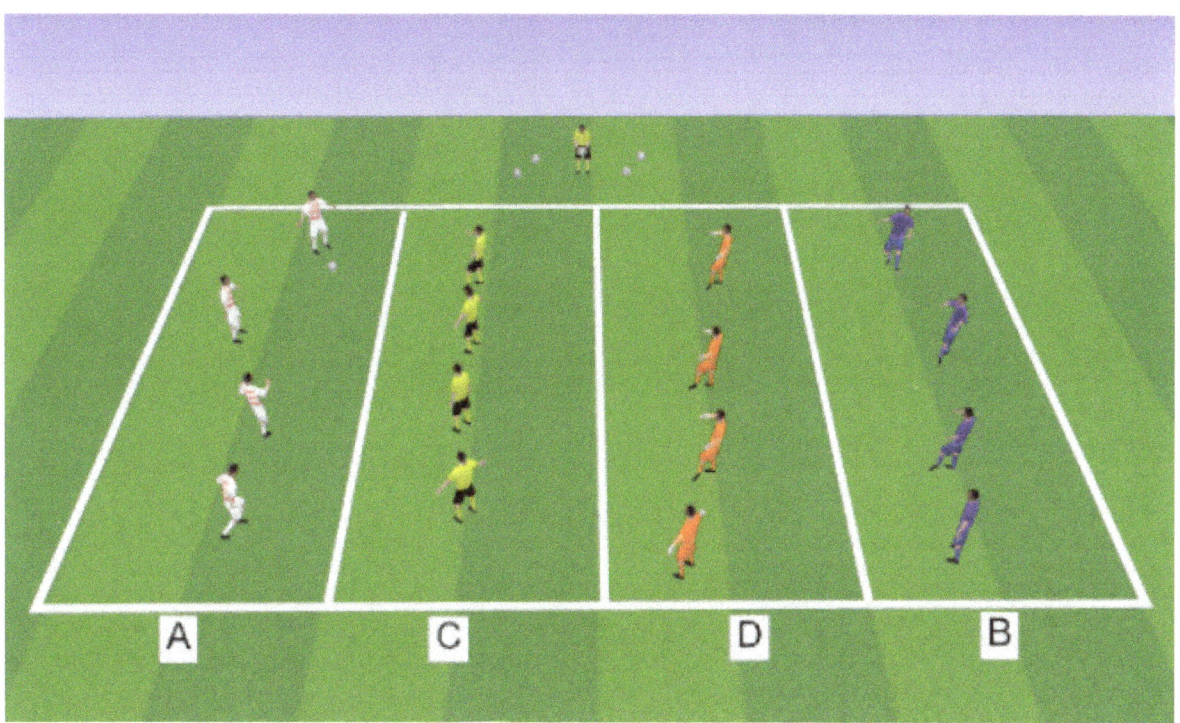

Organisation

40 x 40 yard box, divided as shown.

Four equal teams (play all strikers/attacking midfield players on the same teams).

A good supply of balls at halfway.

How to Play

Team A try to keep possession until they can find a line-breaking pass to Team D.

Team C try to win the ball back and turn and play to Team B.

Continue from Team B to Team C; if Team D win the ball, they play to Team A.

Four x two-minute rounds – rotate teams through each channel.

Progressions (Adjustments)

One player at a time can press their direct opponent in front of them.

Chapter 5

Possible Coaching Points (Focus Area)

- Recognise cues and triggers.
- Lateral movements to prevent gaps.
- Angles and distances of cover.
- Direction and angle of press.

Defending from the front (25 mins)

Organisation

Set up as shown.

Team B has seven players – four defenders (two centre-backs, two full-backs), two midfield players, and one striker; Team A has two forwards (at each end) and three midfield players.

8s and 9s play in their respective shaded areas and the midfield zone (not opposite shaded area).

How to Play

Play starts from the goalkeeper to Team B. The team must try to combine to get the ball to the opposite goalkeeper.

Defending in the Attacking Third (High Press)

Full-backs do not have to stay in the channel.

Goalkeeper should try to distribute to one of the central defenders (conditioned start).

Team A's forwards should attempt to slow down/prevent Team B from playing forward.

If Team B can regain the ball, they counter at the goal with the 7, 8, 9, 10 and 11.

Possible Coaching Points

- Attitude to transition (defence to attack).
- Shape of run (make play predictable).
- Secondary defenders (angles and distances of support).
- Cues and triggers to press.
- Condense the space.

Attack v Defence (25 mins)

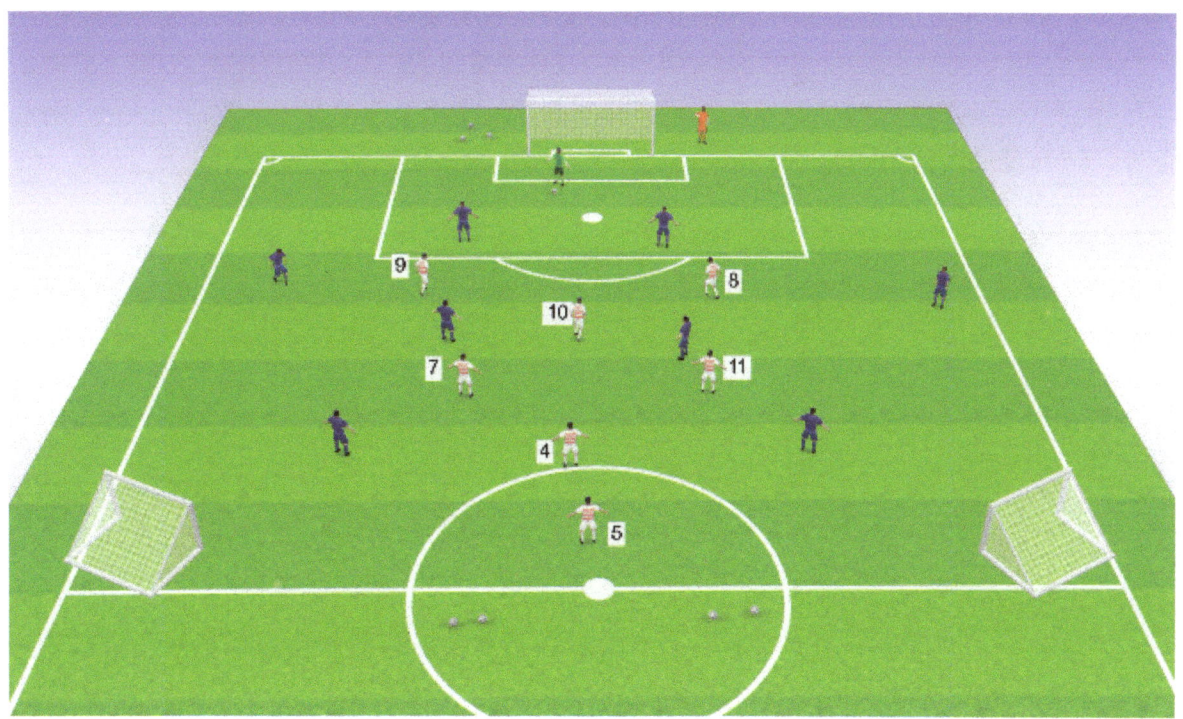

Organisation

Pitch and teams set up, as shown.

Chapter 5

How to Play

Play starts with the goalkeeper (mainly).

Team B play to the two mini-goals.

Team A try to score on the big goal.

Possible Coaching Points

- All those previously mentioned within the game situation.

Practice 3

Pressing (20 mins)

Organisation

(Area not to scale.) End zones are 20 x 15 with a 5-yard central zone.

Three teams of six.

Defending in the Attacking Third (High Press)

How to Play

Team A start with the ball and must make six passes before transferring the ball to Team C.

Team B work in pairs to spoil possession.

Team that loses the ball become the defending team.

Possible Coaching Points

Out of Possession

- Make play predictable.
- Communicate.
- Desire to spoil possession.

Progression

Allow interceptions in the middle zone.

1v1, 2v2 (20 mins)

Organisation

Approximately 20 x 8 yards (as many grids as you need).

Chapter 5

Players work in pairs.

How to Play

Player A passes to Player B, who has to take the ball into the shaded area behind Player A under control.

Play a set number of repetitions, or time, then change roles.

Possible Coaching Points

- Shut Down – speed and direction of approach, move while the ball is moving.
- Slow Down – last few strides, eyes on the ball, distance from the opponent.
- Sit Down – body weight, knees bent, angle body to try to force direction.
- Show Down – confrontation, win the ball, or delay? Poke or block tackle?

Progression

2v2

Possible Coaching Points

- Communication.
- Show into cover.
- Develop understanding of when to stay tight and when to "pass on".
- Individual points above.

Defending in the Attacking Third (High Press)

Functional Practice (30 mins)

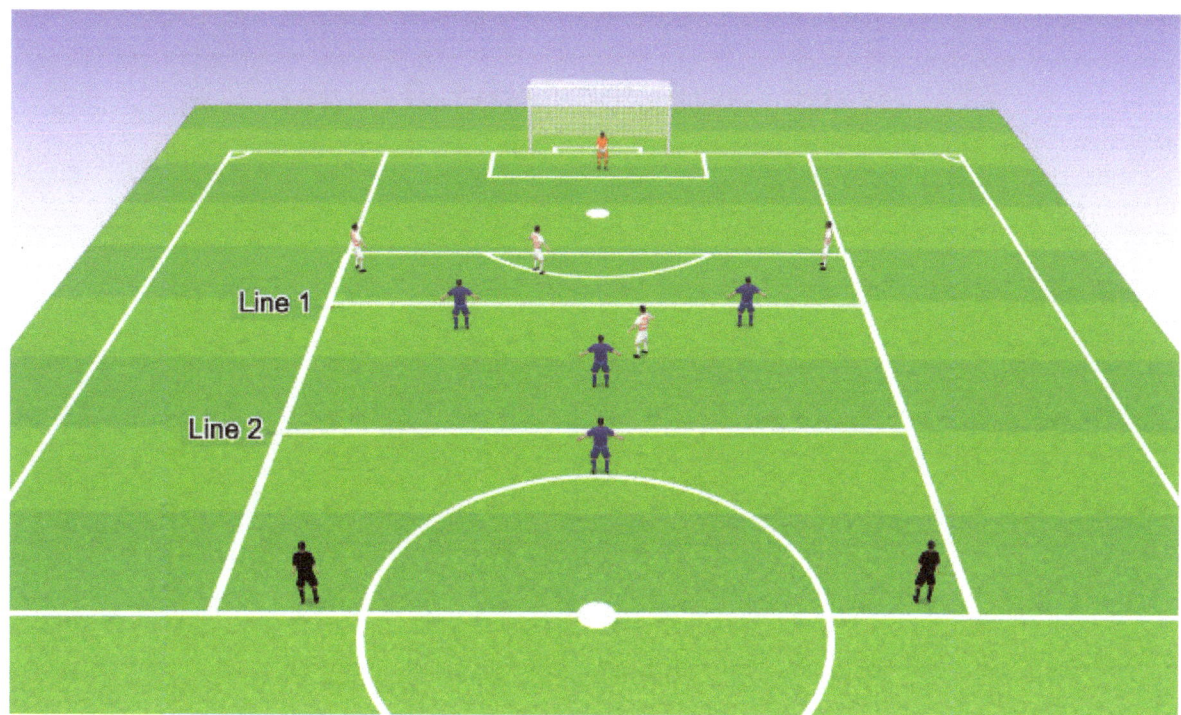

Organisation

Pitch set up as shown.

Line 1 is a pre-determined confrontation line.

Line 2 shows where Team A have to try to get to, before playing to the target players (Black).

How to Play

Play starts with the goalkeeper into a back three.

Team A try to get the ball through the pitch into the two black target players.

Team B try to spoil possession and win the ball back. They then attack the big goal.

Possible Coaching Points

- All points from the technical practices – **the focus is on the defensive element, but don't ignore poor forward play!**

Chapter 5

Practice 4

Warm-Up (Extension) (20 mins)

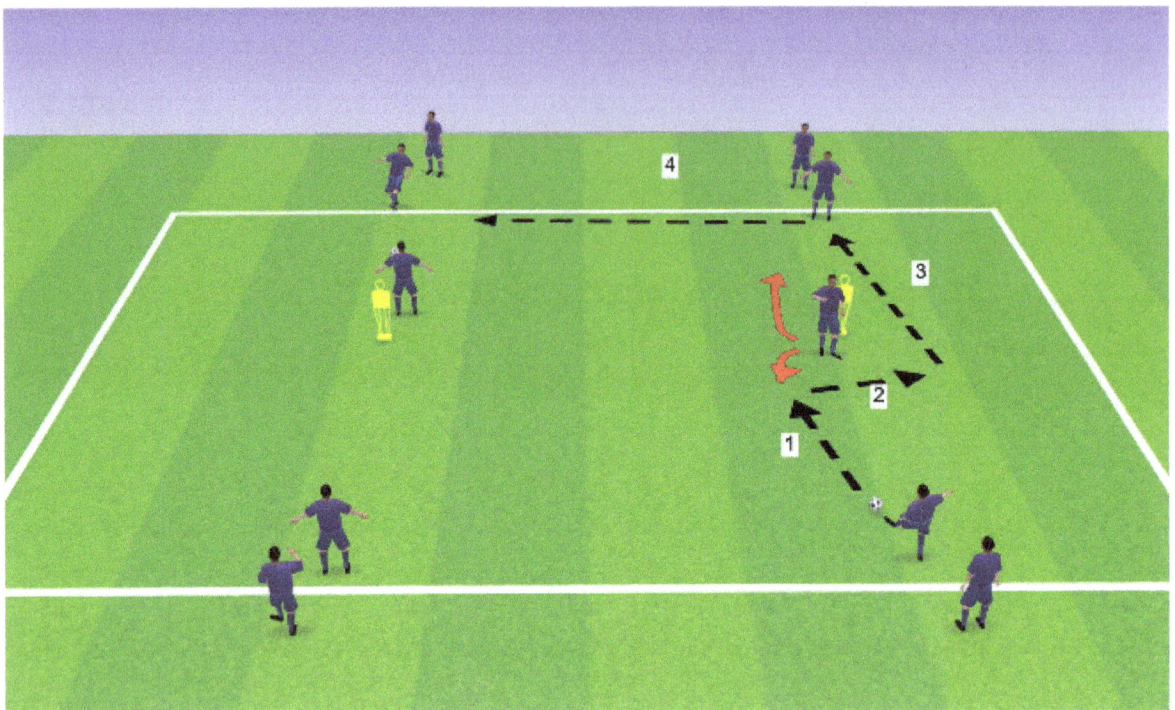

Organisation

Set up as shown, with the mannequins 20 yards from the end lines.

Play starts at opposite points on the outside (two balls in play).

How to Play

Centre player moves off the mannequin to receive the first pass from the outside.

Outside player makes a forward run to receive the ball back and plays out to the opposite end.

The centre player spins out after laying the ball off and runs to the outside.

Progressions

When the ball is passed to the opposite end, it is laid back to the player who was in the middle to play a diagonal ball to the other line.

Use one ball, outside players play into the middle and make overlapping runs; the two central players combine and lay off to the overlapping runners to play out.

Defending in the Attacking Third (High Press)

(They then take over the central positions and play continues from the opposite end).

Press and Transition (20 mins)

Organisation

40 x 40 yard box with a dividing line.

Two equal teams.

A good supply of balls at halfway.

How to Play

Team B try to keep possession 5v2 (adjust numbers to suit).

Team A try to win the ball back and play it back to their teammates.

If successful, they return to their half and Team B send two players in to win the ball back.

Chapter 5

Progressions (Adjustments)

If the team in possession are having "too much" success, send another defender across.

If the defending team get any touch on the ball, the coach feeds a new ball into their half, and the transition occurs at that point.

Defending from the front (30 mins)

Organisation

Set up as shown. Numbers dictate the size of the area (could use full width).

Team B has three defenders and a midfield player. Team A has two forwards and two midfield players.

How to Play

Play starts with the coach serving a ball into the box from a wide position.

Strikers attack the cross if it is possible to do so.

The goalkeeper should try to catch the cross and try to distribute to one of the three defenders (conditioned start).

Defending in the Attacking Third (High Press)

Team A's forwards should attempt to slow down/prevent Team B from playing forward.

If Team A can regain the ball, they counter-attack at the goal.

Team B try to score on the opposite goal.

Possible Coaching Points

- Attitude to transition (attack to defence).
- Shape of run (make play predictable).
- Secondary defenders (angles and distances of support).
- Cues and triggers to press.
- Condense the space.

6
Counter-Attacking (Regains in the Attacking Third)

> "At Barcelona, the first coach that put me on alert to counter-attacks was Mourinho, with Di Maria, Bale, Benzema."
>
> **Pep Guardiola**

Practice 1

Activation/Mentality (20 mins)

Chapter 6

Organisation

Area approximately 20 x 40, with a 3-yard channel in the middle.

Three teams.

Good supply of balls.

How to Play

Team A must make a minimum of three passes before transferring the ball to Team C (the ball cannot be intercepted in the middle zone).

Two players from Team B can try to win the ball back but cannot enter the end zone until the ball has been touched.

If Team B win the ball, the coach feeds a new ball into the opposite end.

Teams play as the defence for four minutes each.

Progression

The defending team changes each time they win the ball.

The defending team can intercept in the middle zone.

Possible Coaching Points

Possession teams

- Passing and movement
- Support play
- Decision making

Defending team

- Working as a pair
- Making play predictable

Counter-Attacking (Regains in the Attacking Third)

Double Value Goals (25 mins)

Organisation

Pitch set up as shown.

8v8 in a 1-3-2-2 formation.

How to Play

Goalkeeper must start play with a short pass (inside Line 1).

If either team regains the ball in the attacking third and scores, that goal counts double.

HOWEVER, they are permitted to play anywhere and if the ball comes out of the attacking third, for a score, it just counts as one.

The team that scores, starts the next play from their goalkeeper.

Possible Coaching Points

- Focus is on the attacking team.
- Set traps.
- Recognise pressing triggers.
- Front two stop forward passes.
- Midfield go tight on their opponent and anticipate the next pass.

Chapter 6

- Defenders push up and squeeze the space.
- Try to quarter the pitch (compress the available space so that only a quarter of the pitch is available for the opposition to play in.

If Team B regain possession

- Secure the ball.
- Can you be direct?
- Run/pass forward.
- Support ahead of, and behind, the ball.

SSG (25 mins)

Organisation

Remove markers.

Play 8v8.

How to Play

Normal rules.

Any regains in the attacking half trigger an 8-second countdown.

Counter-Attacking (Regains in the Attacking Third)

If a shot isn't taken by the time the countdown runs out, the opposition are awarded a free-kick.

Possible Coaching Points

As previous.

Practice 2

Passing and Receiving (15 mins)

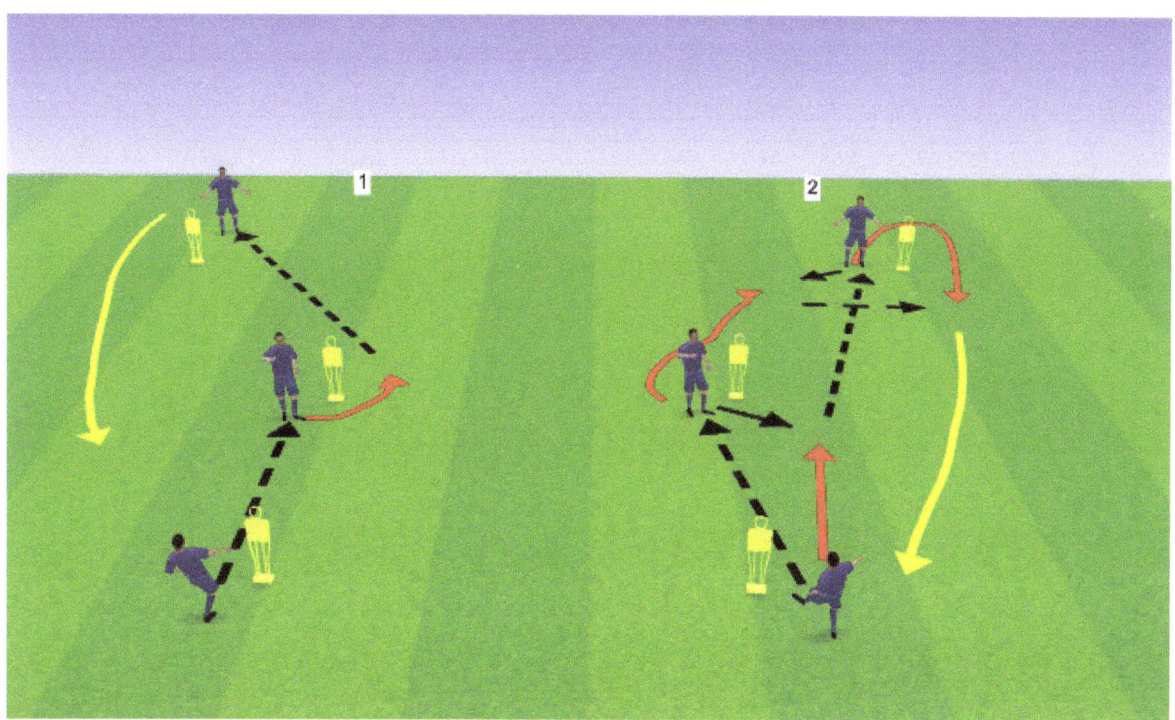

Organisation

Set up as shown, approximately 15 yards between mannequins.

How to Play

1. Pass, touch across the mannequin, and pass to the end man who runs the ball back.

2. Pass, set and spin, play a one-two with the end man who runs the ball back.

Both sides work on 1, then 2.

Work on both sides of the practice to ensure players use both feet.

Chapter 6

Possible Coaching Points

On 1 and 2, passing and receiving techniques, movement off mannequins to create space, running with the ball, body shape.

On 1, reverse passes.

On 2, soft sets, spins, and runs out of the way of the pass.

Possession Boxes (15 mins)

Organisation

Boxes are 12x12 (Championship), 10x10 (Premier League), and 8x8 (Champion's League).

5v2 in each box.

The coach nominates a captain for each box.

After each round, the captain nominates a player to be relegated to a bigger box.

The biggest box nominates a player for "promotion".

Counter-Attacking (Regains in the Attacking Third)

How to Play

10 passes = 2 defenders stay in the middle.

Player gets nutmegged = stays in the middle after he next wins the ball back.

Any defender who gets a touch on the ball swaps with the player who gives it away.

If the ball goes out of play, the defender who has been in the longest swaps with the player at fault for the ball going out.

Quick attacks (20 mins)

Organisation

Set up as shown.

Spare goalkeeper as a target on halfway line to support the team in possession.

How to Play

Coach serves a ball in from the side.

The team winning the first possession tries to complete five passes and can then attack the goal.

Chapter 6

The defending team can win the ball and play to the target player. They then become the attacking team.

After the fifth pass, the attacking team should try to finish the attack as quickly as possible.

Possible Coaching Points

- Quick combinations.
- Positive forward movement and supporting runs.
- Accurate finishing.
- Defensive organisation.

Build Up v Counter Attack (25 mins)

Organisation

Set up the pitch as shown, split into four zones with poles or flat markers.

Two teams with equal numbers of defenders, midfielders, or attackers (or play defenders and midfield v midfield and strikers).

How to Play

Team A has to take a shot at goal within six passes.

Counter-Attacking (Regains in the Attacking Third)

Team B have no restrictions.

Both teams must have all players in the attacking half to score.

Change roles after 12 minutes.

Possible Coaching Points

- Speed of play/actions on turnover.
- First touch or pass forward, if possible.
- Forward runs to support forward passes.
- Team decision – press high to win and counter close to the goal, or drop deep to intercept and break quickly.

Practice 3

Unit Work (30 mins)

Organisation

Area is approximately 25x20 yards.

11 players, no goalkeepers.

Chapter 6

Six x three-minute games.

How to Play

Team A starts with the ball and try to keep possession from Team B.

Team A score a goal for every 10 passes.

Team A can play outside to outside, but outside players are on two touches.

Outside players cannot enter the field of play.

Team B must try to win the ball back and can score in any of the mini-goals.

Coaches are positioned outside the area with a supply of balls to ensure a high tempo and can serve to either team.

Possible Coaching Points

- Team B should try to shape the midfield to set traps to win the ball back.
- Secure the ball with first touch OR play into a goal with first touch (simulate line-breaking forward passes).
- Try to play quickly around the central Team A players.
- Try to create overloads.
- Look for opportunities for one-twos, and third man runs.
- Switch play to a weak side.

Counter-Attacking (Regains in the Attacking Third)

Functional Practice 1 (30 mins)

Organisation

Mark an area of the pitch as shown.

Players organised positionally within the area. (Work from the opposite side with the correct players.)

How to Play

In the shaded area, play 3v2.

Team B try to force a turnover and;

1. Play into the strikers to attack the goal (all Team B join in the attack).

2. Secure the ball and play into the other MF players to play into attack (all players join in the attack/defending).

If the ball comes out of the shaded area whilst Team A are trying to keep possession, Team B can try to win the ball (includes throw-ins).

Possible Coaching Points

- Make Team A play predictably.
- Press aggressively.
- SECURE THE BALL.

Chapter 6

- Play forward – run forward.

Functional Practice 2 (40 mins)

Organisation

Pitch set up and players as shown.

How to Play

Team A try to keep possession in the central area (10 passes = a goal).

Team B try to regain possession and start a counter-attack.

If the ball goes out of the area during possession, the outside Team B players can recover it and counter-attack.

If Team B's central midfielders win the ball, they can start a counter-attack but MUST pass forward.

Team B's wide players stay outside the lines but Team A can go out to defend.

Possible Coaching Points

- As previous practice.

Practice 4

Counter-Attack (25 mins)

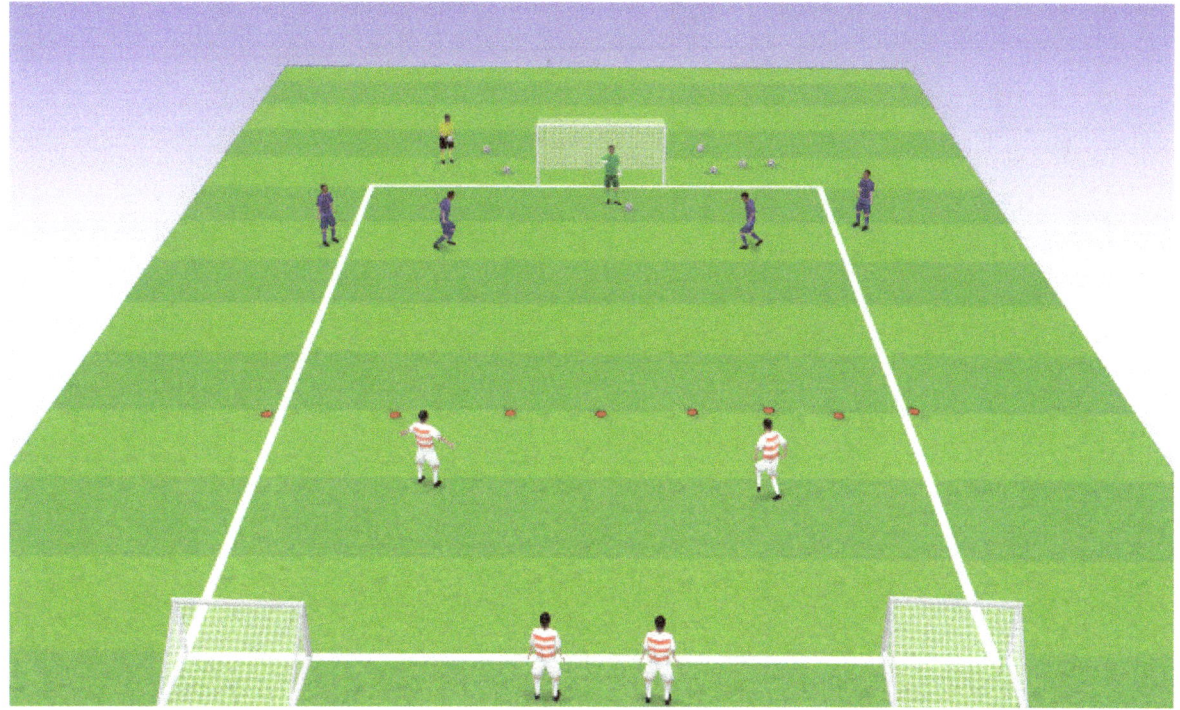

Organisation

The pitch is 25x40 yards with a scoring line marked with flat discs.

Players are positioned as shown.

How to Play

The goalkeeper serves to one of Team B, who must advance the ball past the scoring line and try to score in one of the small goals.

The two Team A players become active as soon as Team B touch the ball and should try to win the ball as high as possible and score in the big goal.

If the ball goes out of play, the coach feeds the next two Team B players to play against the next two Team A players.

Chapter 6

Counter-Attack (25 mins)

Organisation

40x20 with a scoring line 10 yards from goal.

Goals can only be scored beyond the scoring line.

Coach with a supply of balls at halfway.

How to Play

Team A start with the ball and try to score in either of Team B's goals once they pass the scoring line.

If Team A score, the coach plays a ball to the other three Team A players to attack the remaining three Bs.

If Team B win the ball back, or Team A play the ball out, the player who made the mistake must run around the opposition goal and Team B attack with a 3v2. (If the ball has gone out of play, the coach feeds a ball to Team B.)

Counter-Attacking (Regains in the Attacking Third)

6v6 Counter-Attacking (25 mins)

Organisation

Increase pitch size/shape to suit your match day formation.

6v6.

How to Play

Same rules as the previous game.

Possible Coaching Points

- Secure possession (individually or as a team).
- Try to play/run forward quickly.
- Support both ahead of, and behind, the ball.

7

Developing Play Through the Middle Third (Creating the Attack)

> " Football is about having the best offensive play possible. I always like to play offensive football, and nobody will convince me otherwise. "
>
> **Johann Cruyff**

Practice 1

Positional Rondo (20 mins)

Chapter 7

Organisation

Pitch set up as shown.

Players 2 and 3 play outside the boxes to create overloads.

Team B's players are locked into the areas shown.

How to Play

Team A try to advance the ball into the T player through the middle third (no restrictions in the shaded area).

T player moves to support the ball.

Once the ball is with T, coach restarts with a new ball into the back three.

Numbers 2 and 3 cannot play directly to the T player.

Possible Coaching Points

- Recognise and create overloads.
- Speed of play.
- When to play forward, when to retain/recycle.

Progressions

One Team B player can drop into the middle zone to help defend.

When the ball is passed to 2 or 3, they drive inside, and the player who passed out goes to the outside.

Team A can play anywhere, but must retain their team shape from the original start positions.

Developing Play Through the Middle Third (Creating the Attack)

Technical Work (30 mins)

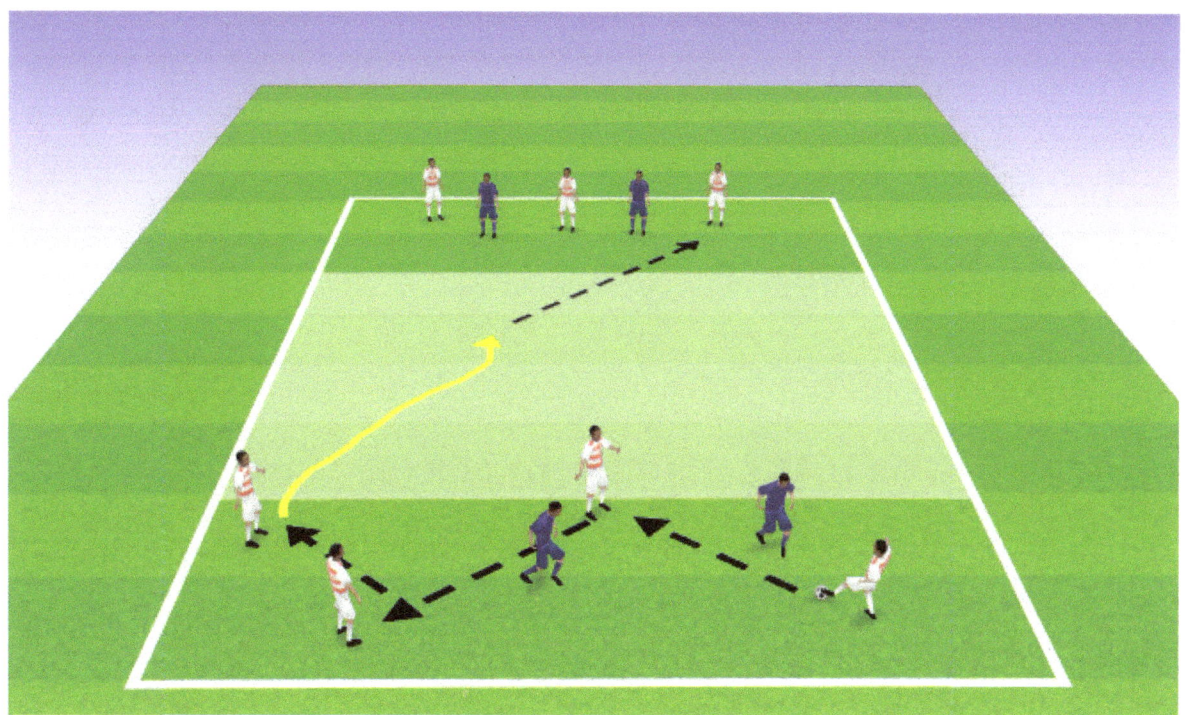

Organisation

Area is 40 x 20 with 10 x 20 end zones.

Teams arranged as shown.

How to Play

The ball starts in the end zone, and Team A must make a minimum of three passes.

One of the players must then break into the neutral zone, at pace, before passing into their team-mates at the opposite end.

Play continues from that end, but the same player cannot make the next run across the neutral zone.

Rotate all players.

Progressions

Allow one of Team B's defenders to chase back.

Allow one of Team B's defenders – from the opposite end – to come out and defend.

Chapter 7

Possible Coaching Points

- Good passing and possession.
- Recognise the moment to break out.
- Good body position to play forward.
- Positive first touch.
- Runs and passes to break lines.
- Create space to receive in the end zones.

Phase-Creating the Attack (30 mins)

Organisation

Organise a pitch, as shown.

Team A play to the big goal.

How to Play

The coach serves a ball to Team A's number 5 or 6.

Play into midfield and combine to play in the forward players to try to finish the attack.

Developing Play Through the Middle Third (Creating the Attack)

If Team B regain the ball, they try to score in the mini-goals from beyond the line.

Possible Coaching Points

- All points from previous practices.
- Support runs for strikers.
- Runs beyond strikers.
- Reactions to transitions.

SSG (20 mins)

Focus on play in the middle third and into the final third.

Neutral players on the outside should help create chances to finish from crosses and through balls.

Chapter 7

Practice 2

Positional Rondo

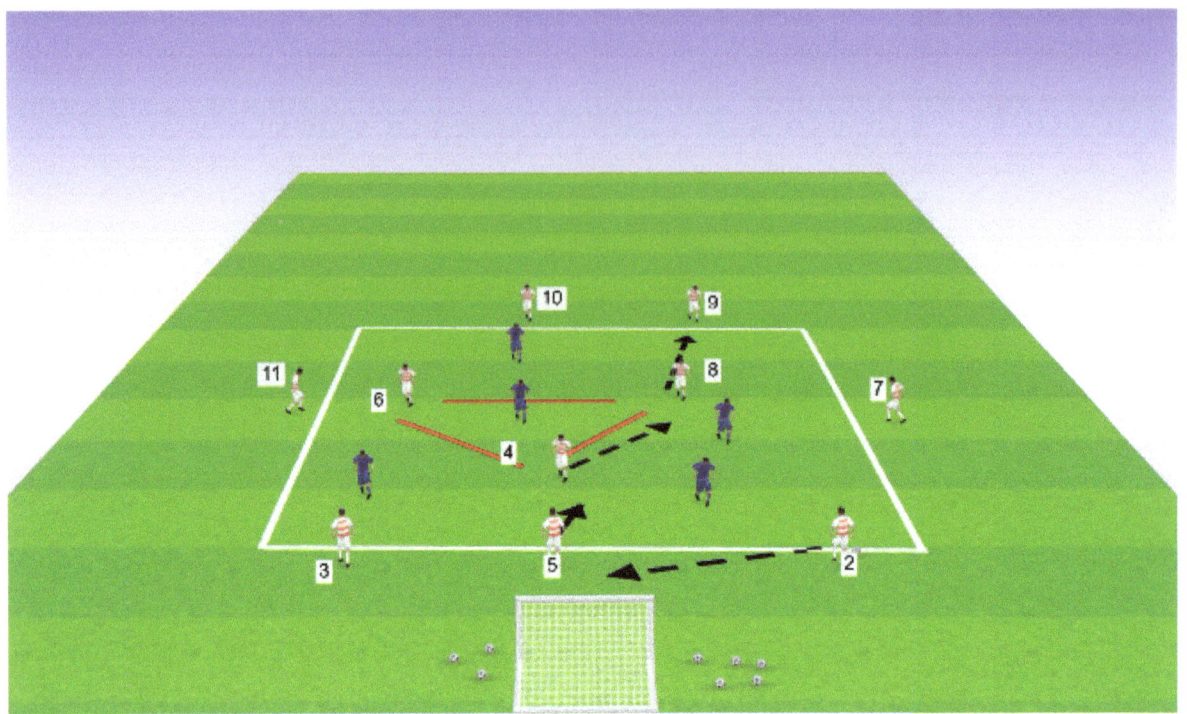

Organisation

10 v 5 in a 30 x 40 area.

A mini-goal 10 yards behind Team A.

How to Play

Team A set up 3-5-2 on the outside, with three midfielders in the middle.

The ball starts from the back three who build up and score by playing to target players number 9 and number 10.

One of the midfielders must play the pass to score.

If Team B can regain the ball, they can score in the mini-goal.

Possible Coaching Points:

- Width and depth of the midfield three (don't block off the lane to the outside pass (7 and 11)).
- Angle and distance.

Developing Play Through the Middle Third (Creating the Attack)

- Speed of play.
- Weight/accuracy of pass.
- Support play.

Squad Practice

Organisation

Set up a goalkeeper and your defensive unit depending upon how your team sets up (back three or back four).

With three midfielders in the shaded area, set up the same in the opposite half.

Both sides work at the same time.

How to Play

The ball starts with the goalkeeper who plays to number 3, who passes to 5 then to 2. As it reaches number 2, number 4 checks into the gate and passes back to the goalkeeper.

The goalkeeper then repeats this and goes the opposite way for number 6 or number 8 to receive in the gate.

Chapter 7

The aim is for the midfield three to provide width and depth and rotate in and out of the gate, as the ball moves between the central defenders.

Progression

1. Once the ball goes to the wide central defender, the ball is played to a player in the middle gate, who then combines with another midfielder, who passes it back to the goalkeeper to repeat.

2. Once the ball is played to the central midfield player, all three midfield players must combine and play forward to the opposite defensive line (simulate playing to a forward player).

Possible Coaching Points

- Width and depth.
- Weight/accuracy of passing.
- Communication (who goes, who stays?).
- Angle and body shape when receiving.
- Support ahead of the back three (angles and distances).
- Support – try to create triangles and diamonds to give passing options.

Squad Practice 2

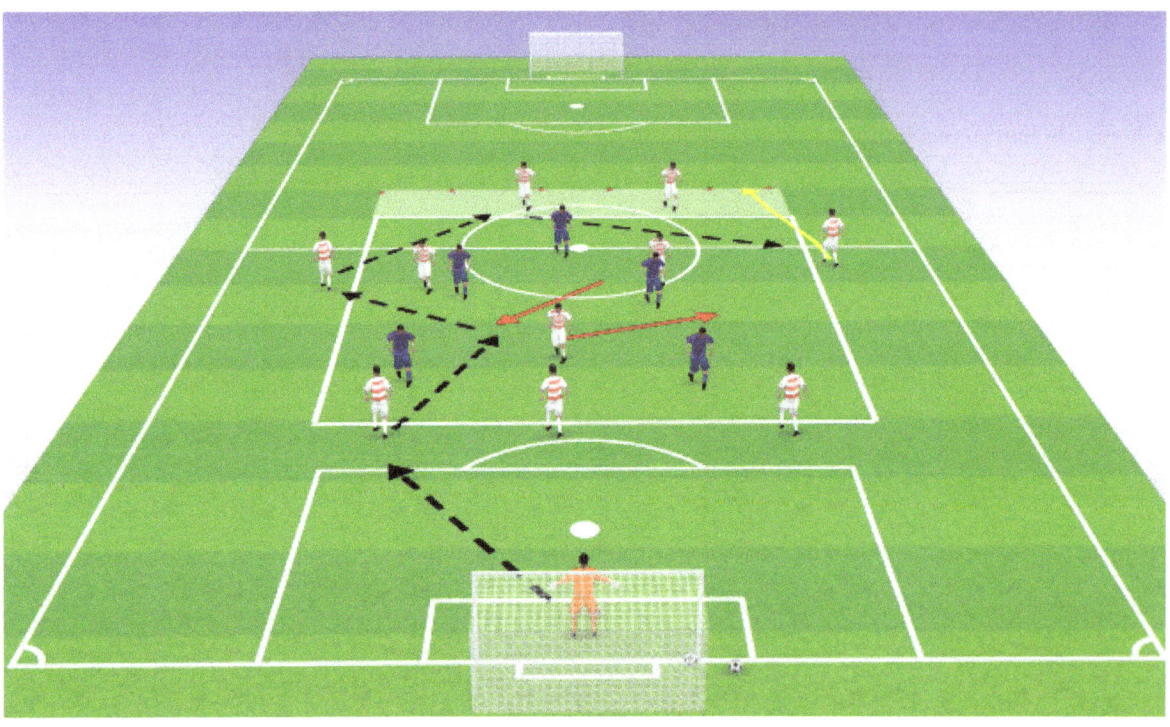

Developing Play Through the Middle Third (Creating the Attack)

Organisation

Progress from the original practice but add a goalkeeper and three target gates.

How to Play

The ball starts from the goalkeeper. Team A score by playing to the number 9 or 10, who then link up with a midfield or wide player to dribble through a gate.

If Team B regain possession, all players break out from the square and attempt to score in the goal.

Possible Coaching Points

- All previous points.
- Defensive transitions.

Practice 3

Attacking Centrally

Set Up

Chapter 7

Organisation

Set up a pitch as shown – it can be scaled down to suit the age of your players.

Defenders from Team A are positioned in boxes, as shown.

3v3 plus two neutral players in a central area.

Coach with a supply of balls at halfway.

How to Play

The Coach plays a ball into the central area, and teams compete for possession.

The neutral players play with the first team to receive the ball.

The team in possession must complete five passes and then attack the nearest goal.

Whichever of the two defensive boxes is entered, the defender becomes active and plays 1v1 to a natural finish (a shot from the attacker or a tackle from the defender).

If the team that starts out of possession win the ball, they can attack in the same way but without needing to complete five passes.

Developing Play Through the Middle Third (Creating the Attack)

Possible Coaching Points

- Quick, accurate passing.
- Movement and angles to receive the ball.
- Pressing to win the ball back.

End Part of the Practice

The attacker breaking into one of the end zones should be positive and finish as quickly and accurately as possible.

If the defender can win the ball cleanly, he can pass out to the coach or into the opposite team in midfield to counter-attack to the other goal.

Possible Coaching Points

- Attackers – positive attitude, changes of pace and direction to unbalance the defender, accurate finishing.
- Defenders – close the space down quickly, try to force your opponent onto his weaker foot, accurate forward pass if he wins the ball cleanly.

Chapter 7

Progression

Team B can all join in the attack to try and score.

Offsides are in play.

Put a time limit on the attack.

Developing Play Through the Middle Third (Creating the Attack)

Practice 4

Passing and Rotation

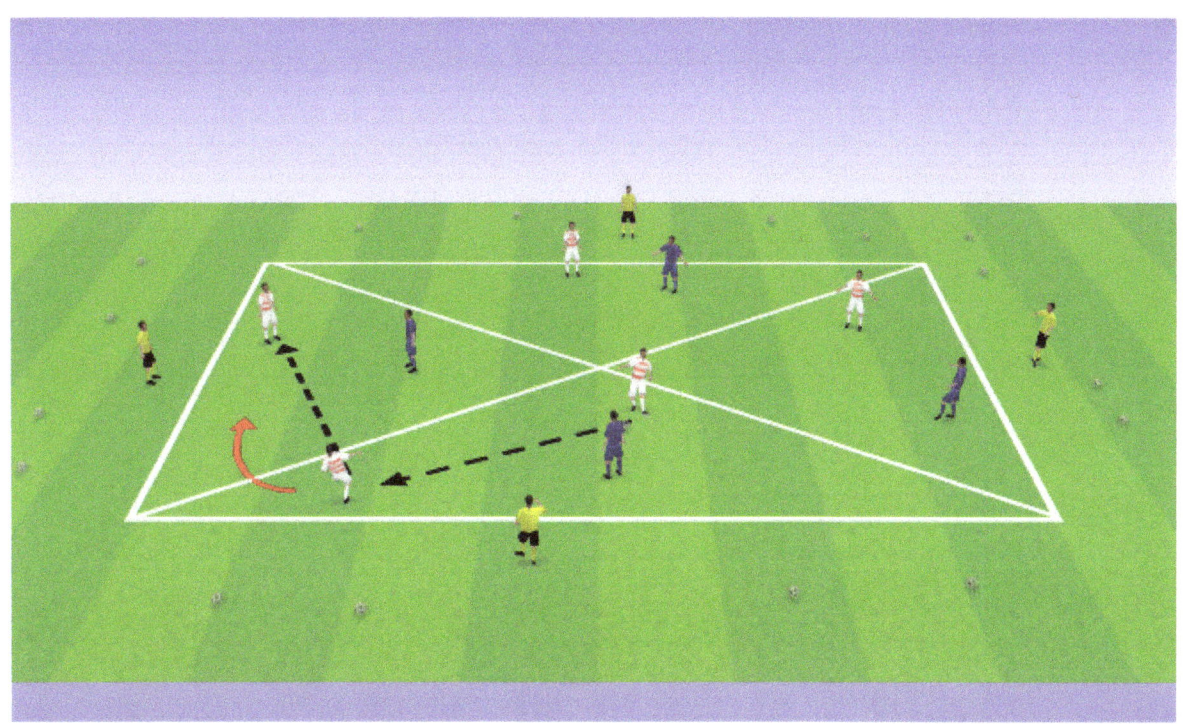

Organisation

Area size to suit the ability of your players but start at 30 x 30.

Divide into triangles as shown, using flat disc markers.

How to Play

Outside players (Team C) are on two-touch.

Both teams in the middle must keep at least one player in each triangle.

Team A (in possession) combine to play the ball into a different area (as shown).

The player who passes the ball out *MUST* leave that area but can be replaced by another player. (He doesn't have to follow his pass as shown in the diagram.)

He *MUST* be replaced by another player.

The player receiving in a 1v1 situation can combine with an outside player or play out to a different area first time.

If he plays out to a different area, he *MUST* leave his area and be replaced.

Chapter 7

Progressions

1. Allow players to run/dribble the ball into a different area.

2. Allow one outside-to-outside pass.

Squad Practice 3

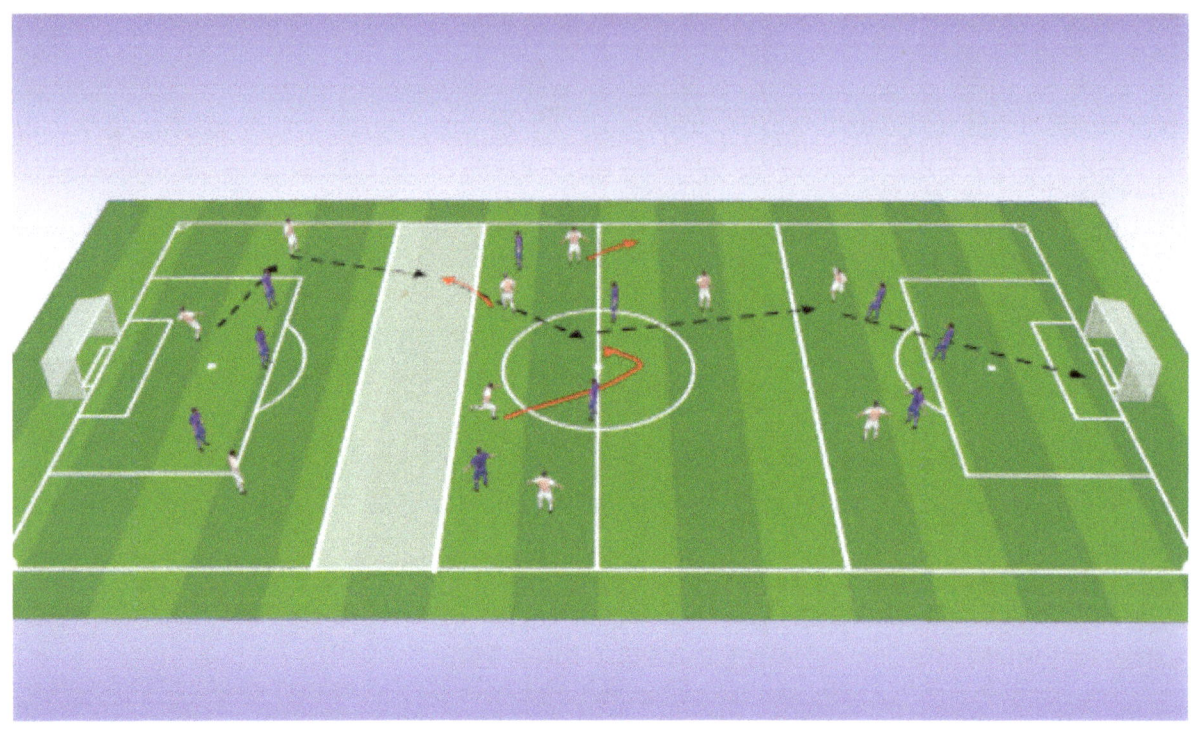

Organisation

Team A starts with the ball, and the team's objective is to score in the opposite goal.

Team B defend and score by getting the ball into their forwards.

All players are restricted to the areas shown to start with.

Only Team A's midfield players are allowed into the shaded area (mark with flat discs).

How to Play

Team A's defenders keep the ball against Team B's attackers until a midfield player drops into the shaded area.

Developing Play Through the Middle Third (Creating the Attack)

If he doesn't receive the pass straight away, he **MUST** rotate out and be replaced by another player relative to the defender in possession.

Other midfield players to move in relation to the holding midfield player in order to support ahead of the ball.

Once the pass has been made out of the shaded area, the midfield players combine to play into the forwards to score.

SSG (shows the movements described in the previous practice).

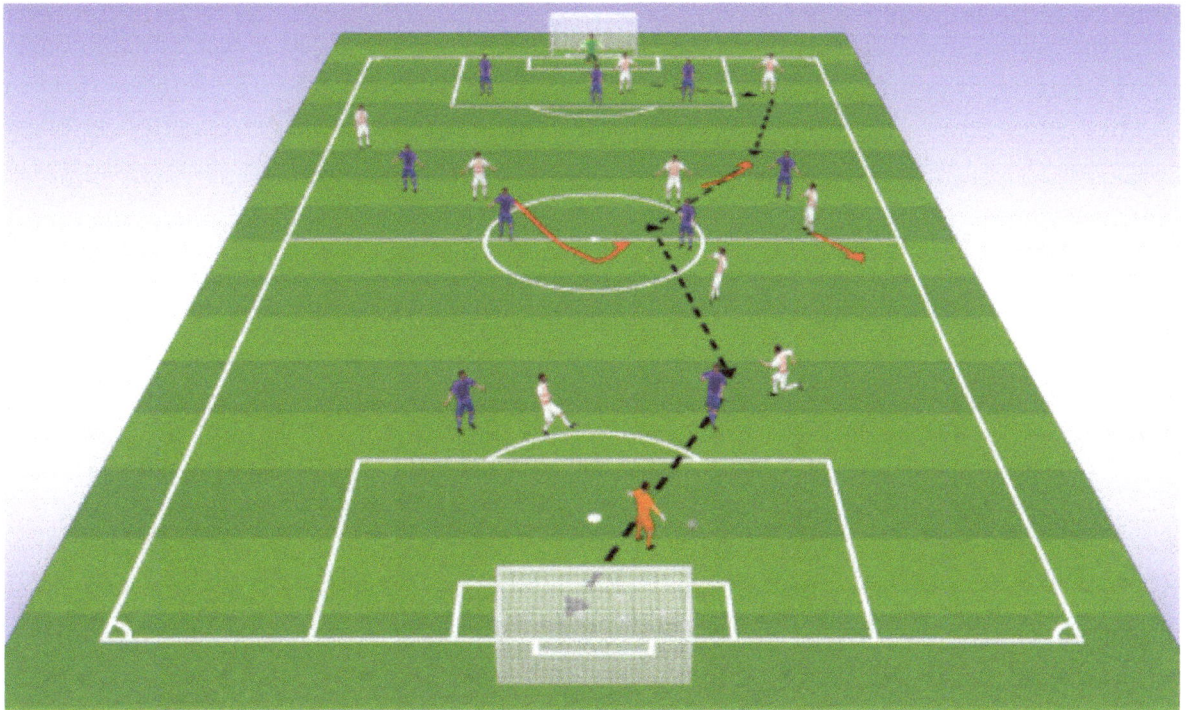

8
Defending in the Middle Third (Medium Block)

> "We want to attack the opponent non-stop when we have the ball, when we lose it, and when the opposition have it. Put another way, defending is our first OFFENSIVE action.
>
> **Jurgen Klopp**"

Practice 1

Midfield Defending Rondo

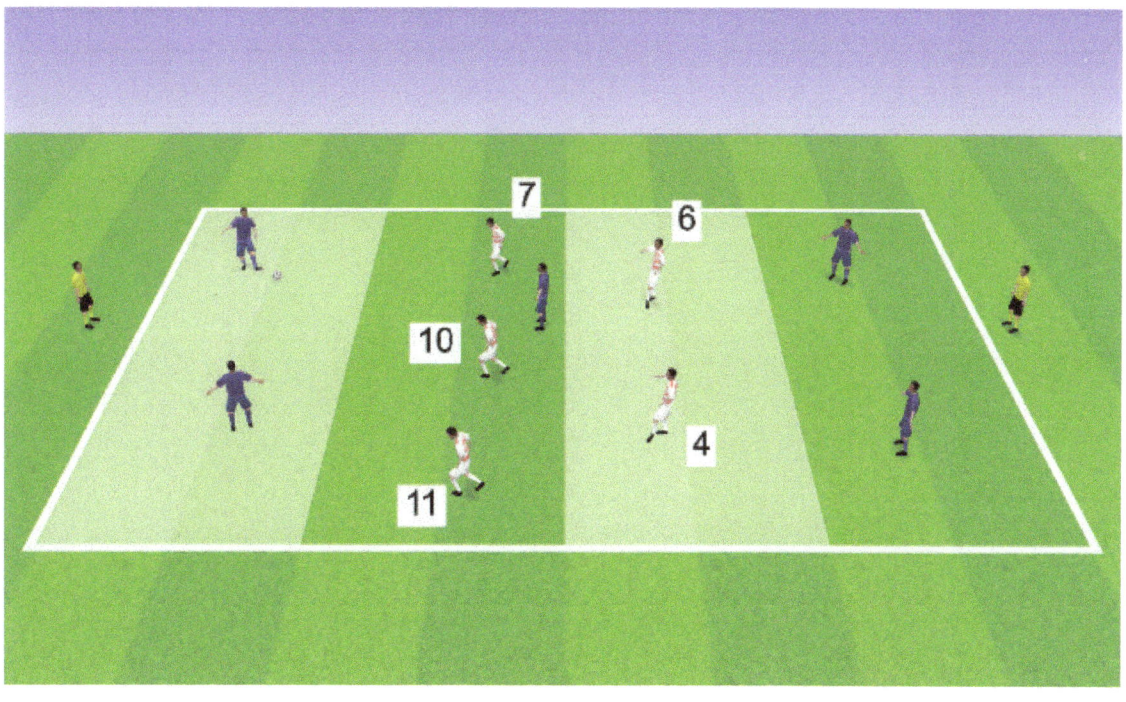

Chapter 8

Organisation

Area is 32 x 20, divided into four zones as shown.

Team A are locked in to simulate the 2-3 midfield in a 1-4-2-3-1 formation.

Team B's player can move anywhere in the middle two zones.

How to Play

Coach plays a ball into Team B who must try to work the ball to the opposite end, via the midfield player.

When the ball goes into the middle zones, one of the deep Team B players can step in to support.

Once the ball reaches the far end, one of Team A moves up to form a three and play is repeated from that end.

If Team A win the ball, they should try to play to the Coach on the outside.

Possible Coaching Points

Positioning and spacing of Team A (4 and 6 cover the gaps between the attacking MF players).

Team A's 7 and 11 show Team B inside – don't allow passes down the touchline.

Press on any poor touch or weak pass from Team B.

Pass to the coach quickly when Team A win the ball.

Defending in the Middle Third (Medium Block)

Technical Practice (30 mins)

Organisation

Pitch and teams set up, as shown.

How to Play

Team B try to advance the ball into the front players and get an effort at goal.

If Team A recover the ball, they should try to pass into the small goals as quickly as possible.

Possible Coaching Points

- Challenging and Intercepting.
- Preventing forward passes.
- Prevent players from turning.
- Defending (body shape and forcing play in one direction).
- Challenging technique (tackling and nicking the ball).
- Tracking runners.

Chapter 8

Phase of Play (30 mins)

Organisation

Pitch and teams set up, as shown.

Mark the angled lines with flat disc markers.

Team A has a goalkeeper, two centre-backs, two central defensive midfielders and one attacking midfield player.

How to Play

Team B try to score in the big goal.

Team A's focus is on the defensive relationship between the spine of the team - two centre-backs, two central defensive midfielders, and the central attacking midfielder.

If Team A regain the ball, they try to play into the small goals.

Possible Coaching Points

From technical points on previous practice.

Defending in the Middle Third (Medium Block)

SSG (25 mins)

Organisation

5-a-side mini-games in the 18-yard box.

1. Goals scored from midfield regains count double.

2. No backwards passes allowed.

The smaller area will allow reinforcement of the coaching points and encourage teams to play forward quickly.

Chapter 8

Practice 2

2 v 2 (15 mins)

Organisation

Each area is a 10 x 20 grid, use as many as required.

Players are organised into pairs. As closely as possible, use players who play next to each other on the pitch.

How to Play

Team A pass to Team B who try to take the ball over the line behind Team A.

Work in pairs to defend and recognise which player needs to press and which player covers.

Possible Coaching Points

- Close the space down quickly.
- Angled run to prevent forward play.
- The pressing player should try to show his opponent towards his team mate.
- Angle and distance of the covering player to prevent a through ball.
- Covering player ready to press if the first defender is beaten.

Defending in the Middle Third (Medium Block)

Progression

Counter-attack to your opponent's line if you win the ball back.

Defending in a mid-block (Midfield Unit Work) (30 mins)

Organisation

Area is 45 x 30.

Set your midfield up in your team shape (Team A part of a 1-4-2-3-1. Team B part of a 1-4-3-3).

Mini-goals on each end line.

Equal teams with no GKs.

How to Play

Team A must retreat into the middle third when Team B starts from their goal.

The defending team can only win the ball in the middle third or their own defensive third.

Teams can only score in the attacking third.

Chapter 8

Possible Coaching Points

- Body shape to defend – play on the front foot to try to win the ball.
- Use the back foot to block tackle.
- Body shape to dictate play.
- Fast feet to match the pace and stride of the attacker.
- Show the attacker into the block to win the ball.
- Counter-attack with pace and purpose.

SSG (25 mins)

Organisation

Same area with full-size goals and keepers.

How to Play

As much free play as possible.

Emphasis on winning the ball in the middle third.

Possible Coaching Points

- All previous.

Defending in the Middle Third (Medium Block)

Practice 3

Warm-Up (15 mins)

Defensive Specific

Players are approximately 8-10 yards apart.

Player A passes to Player B and closes them down.

B advances forward and A jockeys backwards four to five yards.

A passes to B, who lets the ball go through his legs, B turns and retrieves the ball and screens it while A jockeys.

Switch roles.

Progression

Set a cone behind the passer (A) for the attacker (B) to try to get the ball to, which the defender must protect.

Possible Coaching Points

- Close down (quickly).
- Slow down (last few strides).

Chapter 8

- Sit down (bent knees, weight distribution).
- Showdown (try to seize the initiative).

Midfield Block

Organisation

30 x 40 area, lined as shown.

How to Play

Team A (white) has five players trying to prevent Team B (blue) from playing into their target player.

Team A's centre-back provides information from behind.

If they win the ball, Team A play to their target player.

If a player from Team B, in the central zone, drops into the nearest zone to a passer, Team A must decide whether to send a player to press the ball or remain compact.

Defending in the Middle Third (Medium Block)

Whole (20 mins)

Organisation

Pitch size and numbers to suit your group.

Attack v Defence – Team A has a goalkeeper, a back three, and five midfield players v Team B with four midfielders and two forwards.

How to Play

Game-realistic.

Team B try to score past the goalkeeper.

Team A try to defend above the line and win the ball back.

Possible Coaching Points

- Defensive mentality.
- Communication.
- Spacing.
- Decision making.
- Awareness of danger (Threat to goal).

Chapter 8

Part (1) (20 mins)

Looking at defenders' ability to defend the side of the pitch that play is on.

Organisation

Pitch is divided into five vertical zones with flat markers.

How to Play

Encourage Team B to use the width of the pitch.

Team A should remain compact and defend one side of the pitch.

Do not allow the wide player on the opposite side to drag the left centre-back or right centre-back out of shape.

Only need to defend four of the five zones across the pitch.

Opposite side wing-back uses the far post as a positional marker (don't get too narrow).

Midfield to provide cover and protection and be the first to press in order for the defence to keep their shape.

The opposite attacking player is not a threat without the ball.

Defending in the Middle Third (Medium Block)

Possible Coaching Points

- Who closes down, and where?
- Speed of closing down.
- Good communication needed.
- Where to show player in possession?
- When to try to intercept or tackle.
- Emergency defending (put bodies on the line to protect the goal and block shots).
- Out of possession players have two jobs in mind – mark your man and track runners or pass them on.

Part (2) (20 mins)

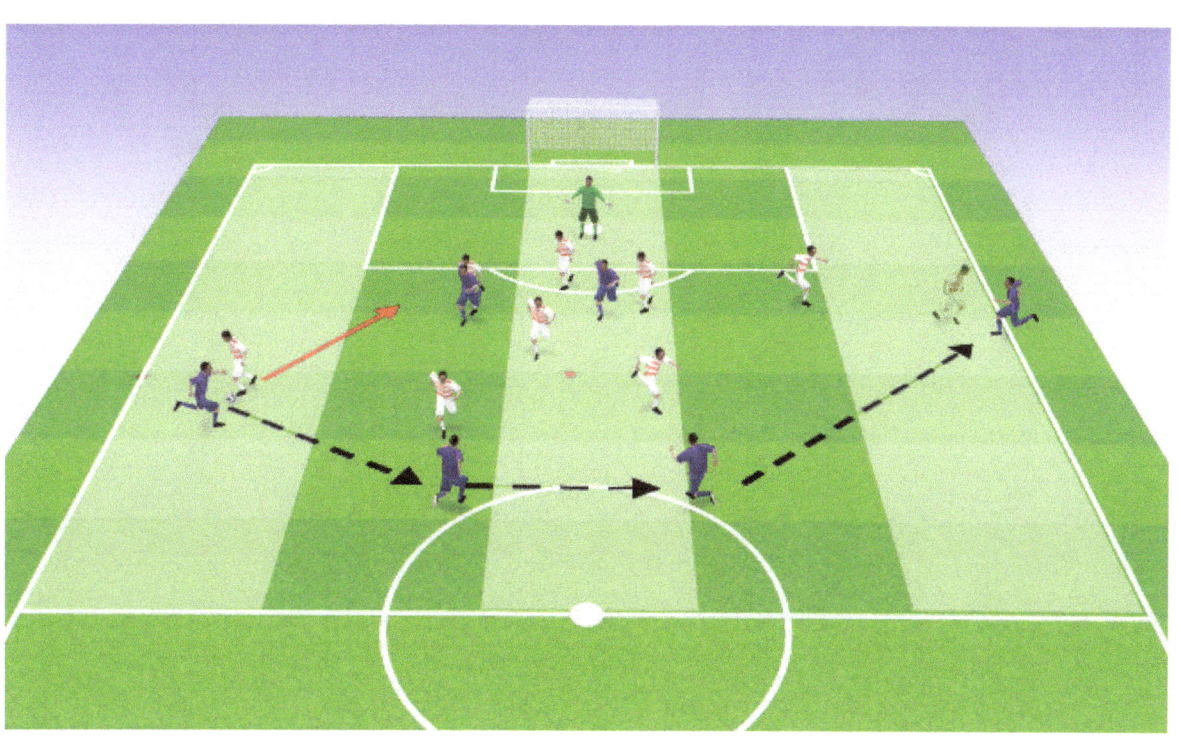

Possible Coaching Points

As the ball is moving (across the pitch), all the defenders should be moving.

Midfield and centre-back shape their bodies to try to force the ball wide, but remain alert to shots from the centre-forward or centre-midfield player.

Goalkeeper communicates to try to keep a high line.

Chapter 8

Whole (20 mins)

Free play in a normal game situation.

Defenders should take the knowledge gained and worked on, in the technical parts of the session into the game.

Working on defensive principles and remaining compact as a unit.

Defending in the Middle Third (Medium Block)

Practice 4

Small-Sided Game (20 mins)

Organisation

A five-yard end zone on both sides of the main playing area.

Team A has target players on the end lines.

Team B has a defender in each end zone, between the playing area and the target players.

A 3v5 (or 4v6) overload for Team A inside the playing area.

How to Play

Play 3v5 (or 4v6) inside the playing area.

Team A pass to their target players to score.

Team B pass to their screening players to score.

Team B should try to screen and intercept as many forward passes as they can, and then attack in the opposite direction.

Chapter 8

Progression

The screening players may press Team A's forward players if they break the back line, but another defender should try to take their place.

Possible Coaching Points

- Screening player needs to be aware of the position of the target player.
- Positioning to deal with impending danger.
- Complete the first pass (retain team possession).

Function (30 mins)

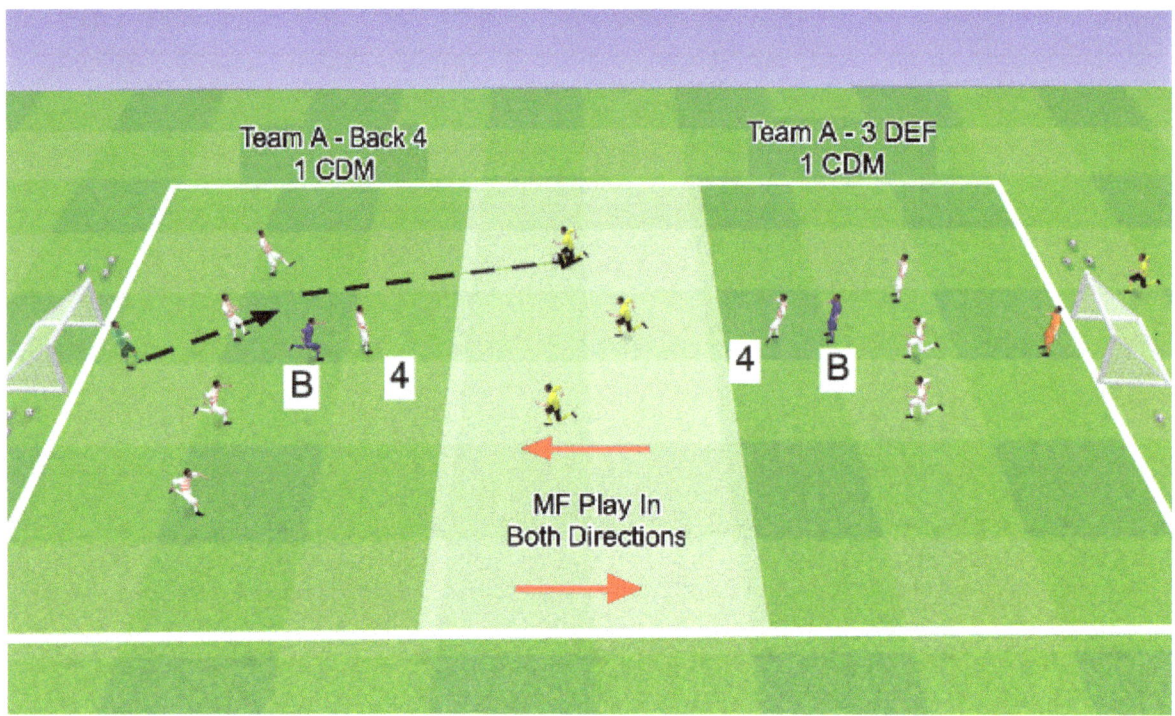

Organisation

Playing area to suit your players (this can be very demanding on the middle three players, so rotate regularly).

Neutral zone in the middle of the pitch.

How to Play

Play starts with the goalkeeper rolling the ball out to a defender who plays into midfield to attack the opposite end.

Defending in the Middle Third (Medium Block)

Midfield players can play into the Forward (B), and all join in the attack to a finish.

If the defenders win the ball, or clear it, the midfield players attack the opposite goal.

Possible Coaching Points

- Screening Player (4) – try to prevent balls into the striker's feet. Shuffle across, and around, in relation to the ball.
- Defenders – block shots! Stay compact when the ball is in central areas. Force play wide or back.
- GK – try to distribute quickly with throws or feet.

SSG (30 mins)

Organisation

Pitch size to suit, with a marked halfway line.

Two teams, equal numbers.

Three-touch limit if you need to increase the tempo.

Chapter 8

How to Play

Tackles can only be made in your own half of the pitch.

Goals can only be scored when all of your team are in the attacking half.

Possible Coaching Points

- Try to slide across in front of the attackers to prevent forward passes.
- Encourage defending players to get back behind the ball as quickly as possible.
- Encourage back players to squeeze the play when going forward.

9
Counter-Attacking (Transitions from the Middle Third)

> "…training has to be as close to real match situations as possible. Of all these situations, one of the most important is transitions, being quick to attack and quick to defend…"
>
> Unai Emery

Practice 1

Rondo (20 mins)

Chapter 9

Organisation

30 x 20.

Players organised as shown (including goalkeepers as outfield players).

Good supply of balls to keep the momentum of the practice high.

How to Play

Team A make a minimum of three passes before trying to pass into the next zone.

Team B try to disrupt play (keep the ball among themselves if they win it cleanly).

Work the ball from end to end, via the middle zone, as quickly as possible.

Possible Coaching Points

- Speed of passing.
- Movement off, and ahead of, the ball.
- Body shape when receiving (can you play forward?).

Progression

Remove the three pass restriction.

Transition Practice (25 mins)

Counter-Attacking (Transitions from the Middle Third)

Organisation

Pitch set up as shown, approximately 40 x 25 yards.

Players organised so that two are resting, two are deep, and two are high.

How to Play

Team A's goalkeeper rolls the ball out to the defenders (Team B's forwards are passive).

Team A must play into their strikers quickly, then support the attack (4v2). Team B's defenders must defend aggressively.

If Team B win the ball, they can play into their forwards and support. (Maximum of one attack in each direction, per play.)

When the play is over (two attacks, or a goal), forward players leave the pitch to the rest position, and other players move up one position.

Possible Coaching Points

- Attitude to play forward.
- Speed of play.
- Speed and angles of support.
- Combination play.
- Finishing.

Progressions

Attacking players increase pressure on the initial pass.

Play to a natural finish (goal or ball out of play).

Chapter 9

SSG (25 mins)

This can be done with your specific positional requirements (Team A would be playing 1-4-2-3-1, Team B 1-4-4-2). Reinforce attacking transition opportunities.

Practice 2

2v2+2 (15 mins)

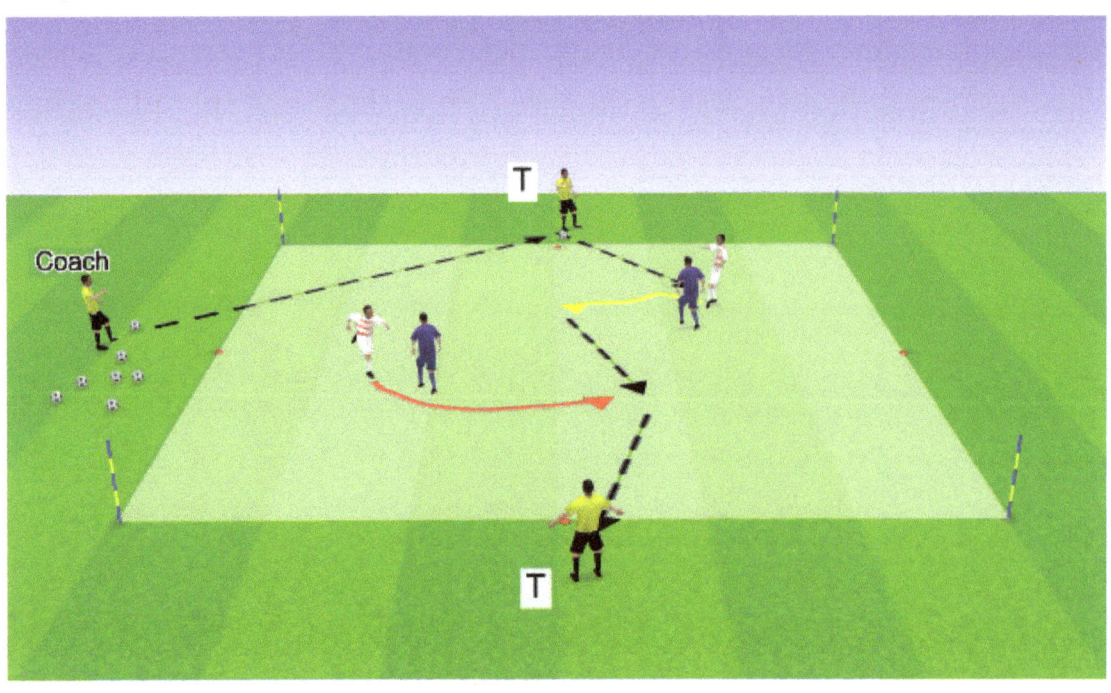

Counter-Attacking (Transitions from the Middle Third)

Organisation

Groups of six players.

2 v 2 plus 2 (two x 24 x 15 yard playing areas)

Two touches for the target players (progress to one-touch when appropriate).

Total of nine games at 60 seconds per game, with players rotating positions.

How to Play

The two players from Team A inside the playing area must try to combine with one another before playing the ball to the target player on the opposite side.

Team B's defenders try to close down the space as quickly as possible to prevent the attacking players from getting the ball to feet.

If Team B wins the ball, there is a quick transition and the game continues.

A point is scored if the team in possession is able to start the play from one target player and connect through the two players on the inside and find the opposite target player to feet.

Possible Coaching Points

- Movement to receive.
- Protect the ball in 1v1 situations.
- Try to combine quickly.
- Pace and accuracy of passes.

Chapter 9

8v4+1 (30 mins)

Organisation

20 minutes (Technical/Tactical)

8v4 plus 1, with transition goals.

Maximum two passes in the end zone, before advancing the ball (2v2 plus 1).

Progress to three passes in the shaded area, before advancing the ball.

Counter-Attacking (Transitions from the Middle Third)

How to Play

Team A is trying to keep the ball from one end to the other, and back. If they are successful in doing so, they score a point.

Team B is trying to win the ball back in the middle zone, then counter-attack to one goal in transition.

Team B do this by playing into their striker and releasing players out of the middle zone to make a 3 v 3 going to goal.

The entry pass from the defenders must be into the middle zone, and into a player of the same colour (not the neutral).

The two players in the middle zone must try to lose their markers, to be available for the entry pass from the defenders.

On winning back possession, the Blue team must:

1. Secure possession.

2. Attack quickly.

3. Support quickly.

Transitions Game (30 mins)

Chapter 9

Organisation

Pitch set up as shown.

Team A start with six players, against four from Team B (with two players at the side of the pitch).

How to Play

Team A attack Team B's goal.

If they score, they restart with possession from their GK.

If Team B win the ball back, the Team A player who gave it away – and one other – leave the pitch and the two Team players on the side **IMMEDIATELY** come on to join the attack.

Practice 3

SSG (15 mins)

Organisation

Pitch is approximately 60 x 40 yards.

Counter-Attacking (Transitions from the Middle Third)

Play a SSG.

How to Play

Normal rules, including offside.

Any goals scored from a regain in the attacking 2/3 of the pitch count double.

NO COACHING.

Counter from own half (15 mins)

Organisation

Area is approximately 50 x 30 yards.

Set up 4v3 plus goalkeeper in one half, against 3v2 plus goalkeeper in the other.

Goals are set 5-10 yards behind the end line.

How to Play

Team A's goalkeeper feeds the ball into the outfield players.

Set a minimum number of passes (depending on ability) before the ball can be played into the forwards.

Chapter 9

Once the ball is played into the forwards, two of Team A can cross into the attacking half to try to score.

If Team B win the ball (or the keeper makes a clean save), they can play the ball directly into their forwards.

Possible Coaching Points

- Think in advance of the play.
- Speed of play.
- Awareness of teammates' positions.
- Think PLAY FORWARD – RUN FORWARD.
- Speed and angle of supporting players.
- Try to finish the attack clinically.

Progressions

Eight seconds to score from a counter-attack.

Allow a recovering defender.

Counter from MF (15 mins)

Counter-Attacking (Transitions from the Middle Third)

Organisation

Divide the pitch into three zones, as shown.

1v1 in each end, with a 3v3 plus two neutral players in the middle.

Neutrals play with the team in possession.

How to Play

Play starts in the middle zone.

Teams have to keep possession for a set number of passes (3-5) before playing into the forward.

One of the attacking players can join the attack to make a 2v1.

If Team B's defender or goalkeeper wins the ball, they can play directly into their forward and counter the other way.

Possible Coaching Points

As previous practice.

Progression

Allow a recovering defender.

SSG (15 mins)

Chapter 9

Organisation

Same as the first part of the practice.

How to Play

Normal rules, including offside.

Any goals scored from a regain in the attacking 2/3 of the pitch count double.

LOOK FOR EVIDENCE OF LEARNING AND UNDERSTANDING.

Practice 4

Positional Rondo (30 mins)

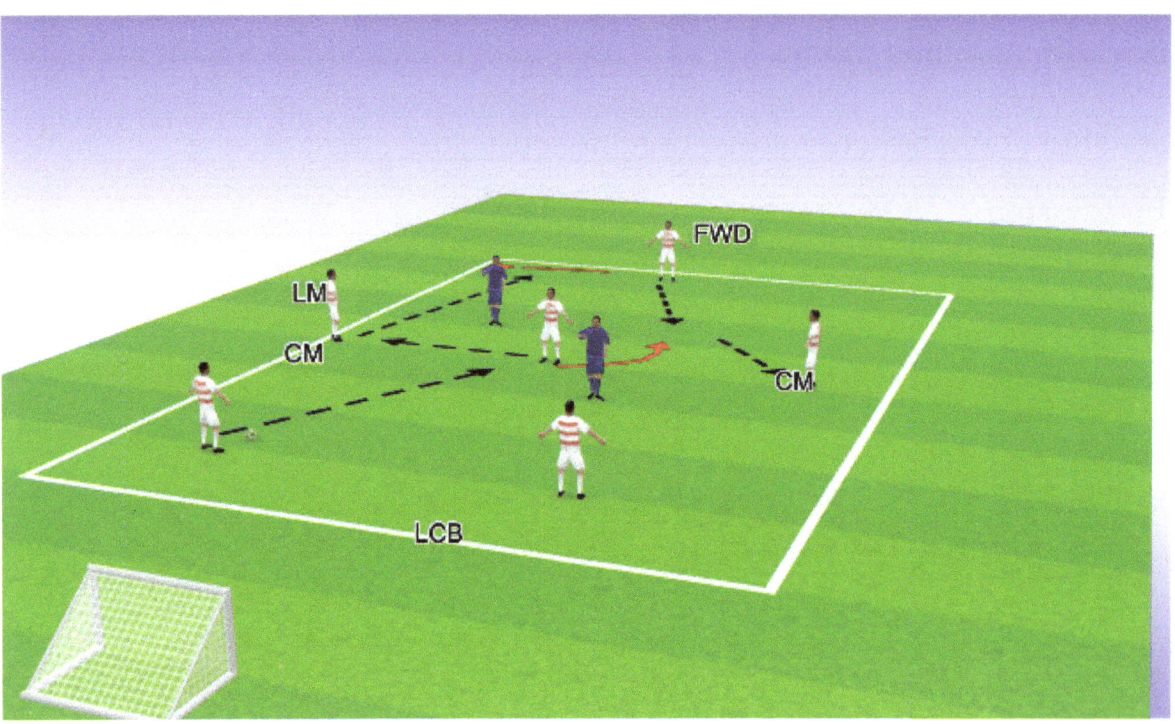

Organisation

This is a position-specific Rondo used to warm up the players in their natural positions.

Score a point every time the MIDDLE player is used to keep possession.

Set up another Rondo with right-sided players alongside.

Counter-Attacking (Transitions from the Middle Third)

Place a mini-goal 10 yards behind the defenders.

How to Play

Try to work the ball from the defenders to the forward player.

Try to play with as few touches as possible.

If Team B regain the ball, they try to score in the mini-goal.

Progressions

Allow the MIDDLE player to rotate with either the left midfield player or other central midfield player.

Possible Coaching Points

- Pace and accuracy of pass.
- Support play.
- Gradually build up the tempo.

Progression 1 (30 mins)

Chapter 9

Organisation

The area is half a pitch.

Team A has two forwards against 3 defenders from Team B in the attacking half.

Team A has five midfield players against 3 players from Team B, in their defending half initially.

Team A's midfield players can only cross the halfway line, after the ball is played forward.

How to Play

Play starts with the goalkeeper rolling the ball out to any Team A midfield player.

They should then try to advance into the attacking half as quickly as possible to get strikes on goal.

Team B restarts after a shot or goal, and attack Team A's goal.

Team A drop off to allow the ball to cross the halfway line.

Progressions

Team A play one or two-touch to change the tempo of the game.

Team B can add a recovering defender when Team A attack.

Possible Coaching Points

- Pace and accuracy of forward passes.
- Timing, angle, and distance of support.
- Game-realistic tempo throughout.
- Team and unit cohesion.
- Attitude to get forward and support quickly.

Counter-Attacking (Transitions from the Middle Third)

Progression 2 (30 mins)

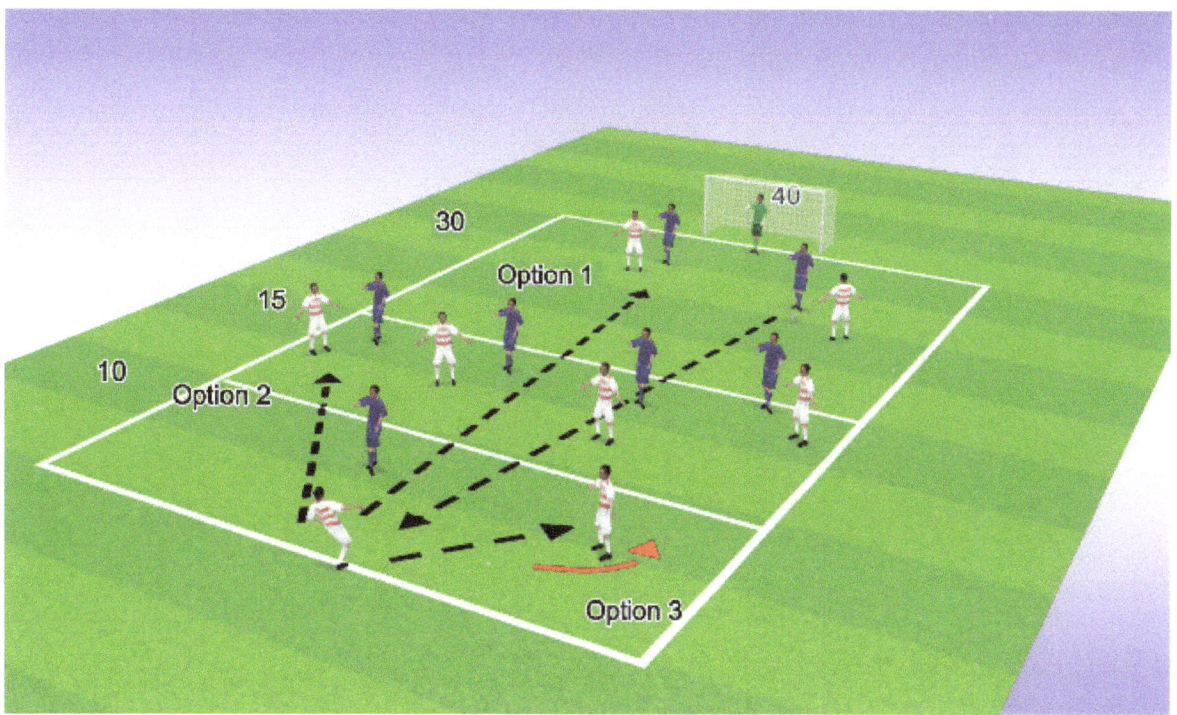

Organisation

Area is 40 x 55 yards.

Pitch set up as shown.

Play starts with Team B's defender playing long to Team A then recovering into a defensive position.

How to Play

Team A should try to distribute quickly and accurately to forward players as shown.

They have ten seconds to try to score.

When the ball goes into the 30-yard area, Team A can send in two midfield players to support the attack.

If Team B regain possession, they should try to score quickly.

Progressions

Challenge Team B to score within six seconds (this should encourage quick turnovers, ensuring Team A get more opportunities to counter-attack).

Chapter 9

Possible Coaching Points

- Movement ahead of the ball to create opportunities to strike.
- Compact defending on transition.
- Speed of movements. (Match tempo.)
- Team/unit work.
- Quick change of mentality to attack.

10
Developing Play in the Attacking Third (Finishing the Attack)

> " Every season is a new challenge to me, and I always set out to improve in terms of games, goals, assists. "
>
> Cristiano Ronaldo

Practice 1

Waves Practice (20 mins)

Chapter 10

Organisation

Pitch and teams laid out, as shown.

The numbers relate to Team A.

Team A's midfield will play in both directions.

Team B will defend and start locked into the three areas.

Two neutral players in the outside channels.

Team Objectives

Team A create opportunities to score from crosses (but don't play unrealistically).

Team B defend effectively in all three zones, and play into the goalkeeper or neutrals if they win possession.

How to Play

The game starts from the goalkeeper playing into the midfield.

As soon as one of Team A's players touches the ball, Team B are "live".

The two neutral players are initially restricted to two touches and must play what they see (cross or recycle).

If Team B win the ball, play directly to the goalkeeper or neutral players **(THIS ENDS THE PLAY)**.

If Team A are attacking towards the top goal, they can also retain possession by bouncing off the opposite number 9 and number 10.

Start the next attack from the opposite end.

Possible Coaching Points

- Midfield rotation to retain possession of the ball.
- Neutral players support in relation to the ball.
- If the Neutral players shape to cross the ball, there needs to be striker movement and MF support runs.
- Recycle if the cross is *not* on.
- If the Neutral player gets into the attacking third – they need to make a decision to cross or cut back.
- Positional adjustments in relation to crosses (high up or middle third).

Developing Play in the Attacking Third (Finishing the Attack)

Progression

Allow a defender into a channel.

Remove touch restrictions.

Game (25 mins)

Organisation

Pitch and teams set up, as shown.

How to Play

Normal rules, including offsides.

Possible Coaching Points

Anything related to topic:

- Overlaps and underlaps.
- Angles of crosses.
- Player movement/adjustments to match the angles of delivery.
- Type and quality of finishes.

Chapter 10

Practice 2

Attacking patterns (30 mins)

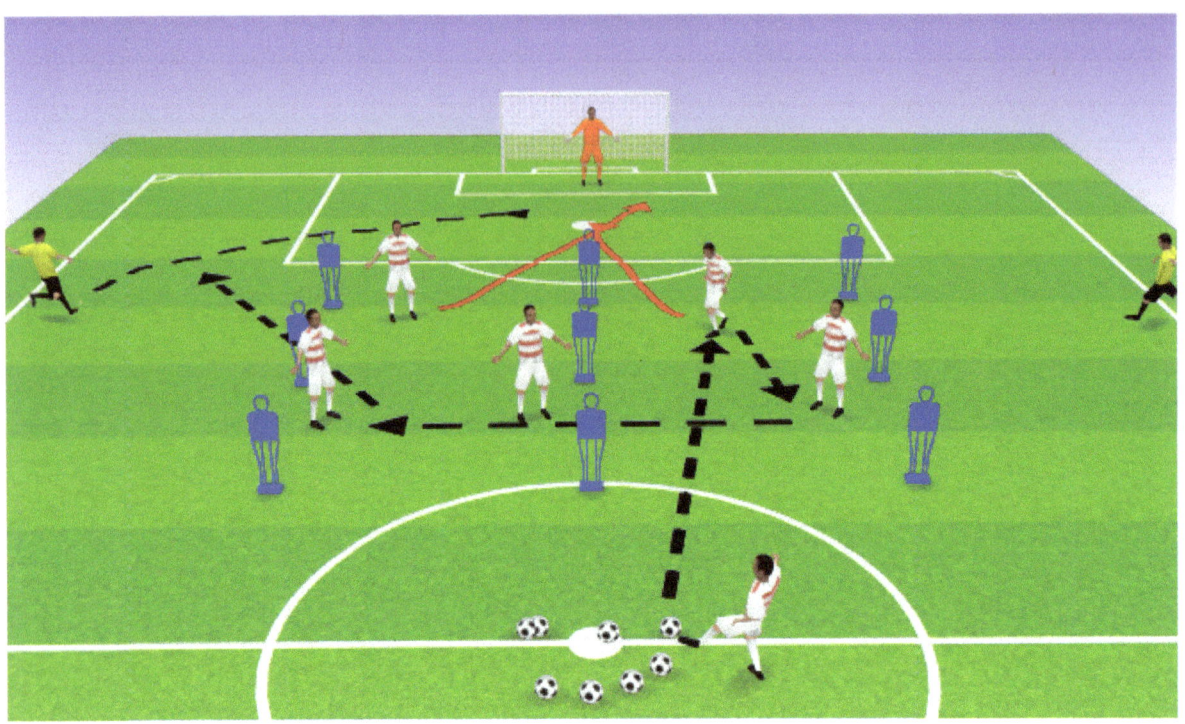

Organisation

The mannequins form a 30-yard square, divided into four boxes. (The boxes are used to keep appropriate space/distances between players).

How to Play

Using a front two, and a midfield three, work on patterns of play and movement between the five players.

Minimal touches.

Holding midfield player starts with a pass into the boxes and remains available to re-circulate the ball.

On the coach's call, the players have eight seconds to create a shot at goal. This can be via the wing-backs or a through ball from midfield.

Possible Coaching Points

- No more than two players in the front two boxes.
- Rotation of midfield three (never all three in one box).

Developing Play in the Attacking Third (Finishing the Attack)

- Quality of touches/passes.
- Communication.
- Quality/pace of balls into the box.
- Accuracy before power on all finishes.

Opposed practice (30 mins)

Organisation

Replace the mannequins with flat markers.

Add in Team B's back four and a midfield three.

How to play

Wing-backs can work the full depth of the half.

Restrict the defenders' movement initially; the midfield three must stay within the width of the boxes.

Back four can only come up to the middle set of cones.

Team A keep possession until the coach's call and then have to score within eight seconds.

Chapter 10

Progression

Free play.

Practice 3

Combination play through midfield to go wide (10 mins)

Half Pitch

Team A – 2 x centre-midfielders, 2 x full-backs, 2 x wide players, 1 x centre-forward

Team B – 1 x goalkeeper, 1 x centre-back, 2 x full-backs, 1 x centre-midfielder.

Pattern

Play starts with Team B's midfielder giving away possession to one of Team A's centre-midfielders.

1. With the centre-midfield player's first touch, pass into the centre-forward and then make a diagonal run into space created by the centre-forward.
2. The centre-forward sets the ball to the full-back, who is advancing.

Developing Play in the Attacking Third (Finishing the Attack)

3. Full-back plays to the winger and makes a forward run to create a 2v1 situation.
4. Wide player and full-back create a crossing opportunity with an overlap or a set-back.

When play breaks down, or Team A score, go down the left side.

Countering with rotation and forward runs. (10 mins)

Pattern

Play starts with Team B's centre-midfield player giving possession away to Team A's midfielder.

The centre-midfield player passes into the centre-forward and runs into forward space, taking the Team B midfielder with him; as he does this, the other centre-midfielder times a run around the back and receives a pass from the centre-forward.

The wide player needs to time his run inside to take Team B's full-back away and allow Team A's full-back to advance forward into space for a cross.

Encourage Team B's full-back to make a decision, either track the winger or go with the full-back; this makes the centre-midfielder's passing decision more

Chapter 10

realistic, either pass into the wide player coming inside for a shot, or the full-back for a cross.

Combination play with third man run (10 mins)

Pattern

Play starts with Team B's midfielder giving away possession to Team A's centre-midfielder.

Team A's centre-midfielder passes into centre-forward.

The centre-forward passes to the full-back. As the pass is going back, Team A's wide player goes wide to drag Team B's full-back away and the opposite centre-midfield player sprints into the space created. His two options are to:

1. Shoot, or
2. Set to the wide player for a cross.

Developing Play in the Attacking Third (Finishing the Attack)

Combination play with switch. (10 mins)

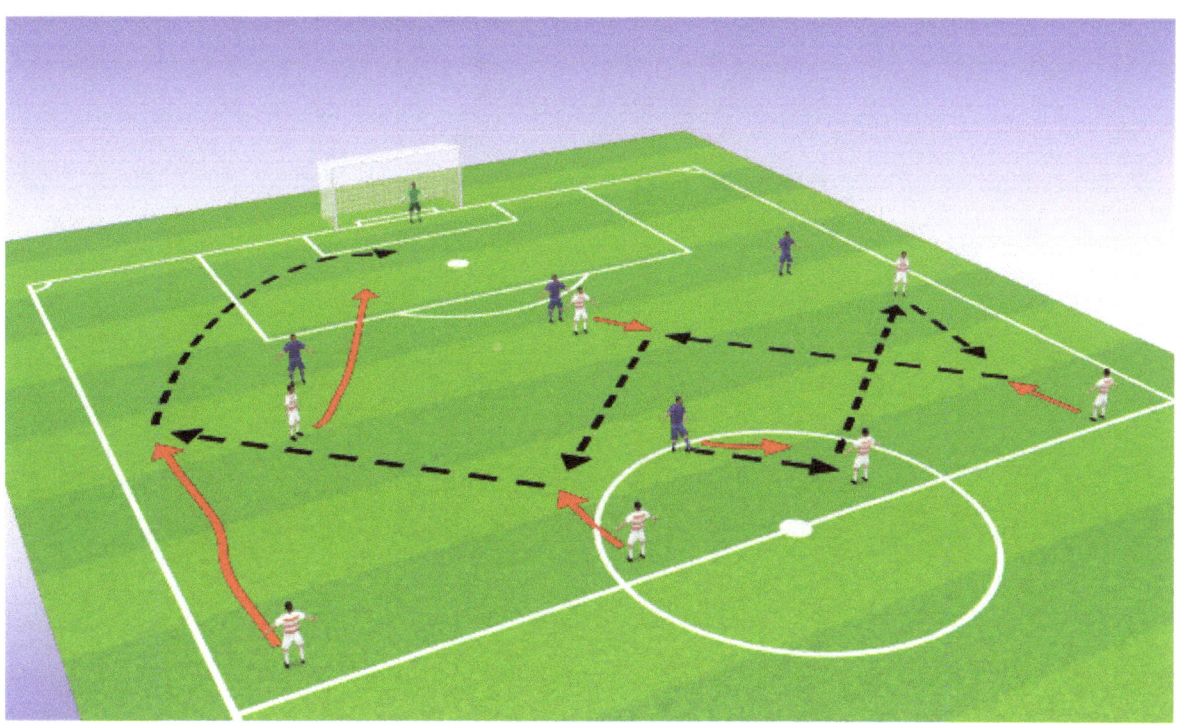

Pattern

Team B's centre-midfield player gives the ball away to Team A's centre-midfielder.

1. The pass then goes into the wide player.
2. The wide player sets the full-back.
3. The pass then goes first time into the centre-forward.
4. The centre-forward then sets the opposite centre-midfield player and, as the ball is set, the other forward runs inside to create space for the full-back to receive a pass from the centre-midfielder and cross the ball.

Chapter 10

Practice 4

Unit Work 1

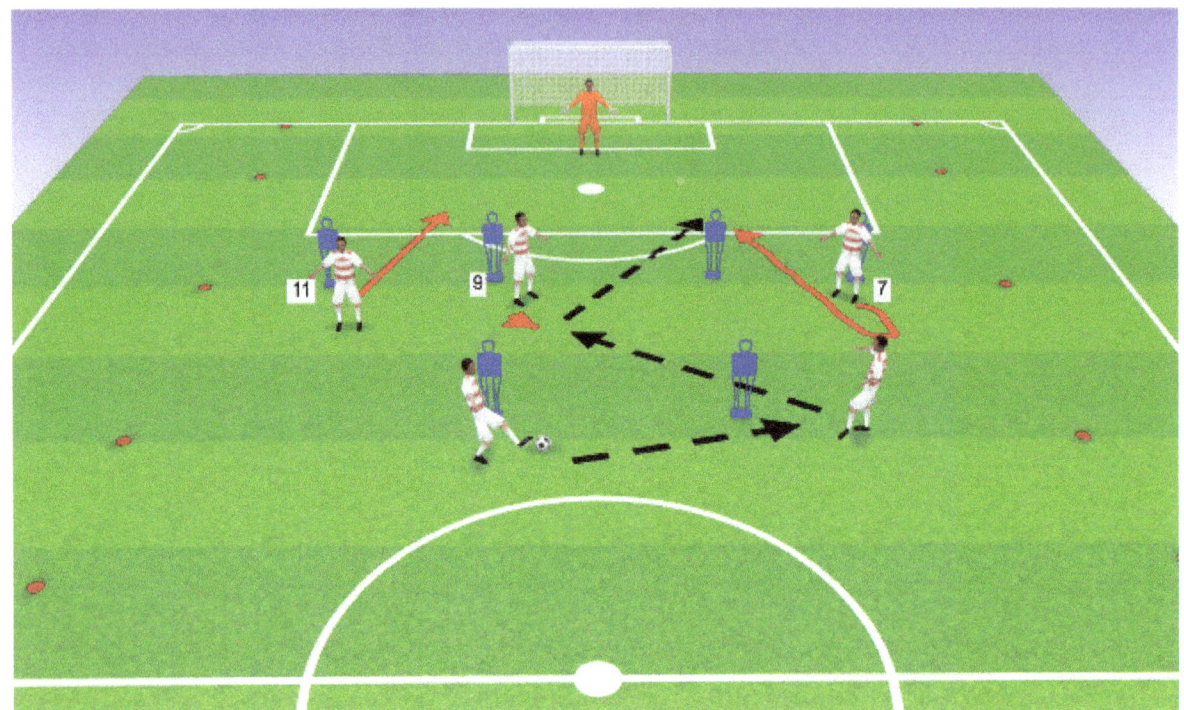

Organisation

Pitch set up as shown.

Have a good supply of footballs.

Start the practice with a square pass in midfield to trigger the forward player's movement.

How to Play

On the initial pass, the forwards move as shown, 9 drops into the space to receive.

7 moves off the defender and makes an out-to-in run for a finish.

11 follows in for rebounds or misplaced shots.

Developing Play in the Attacking Third (Finishing the Attack)

Unit Work 2

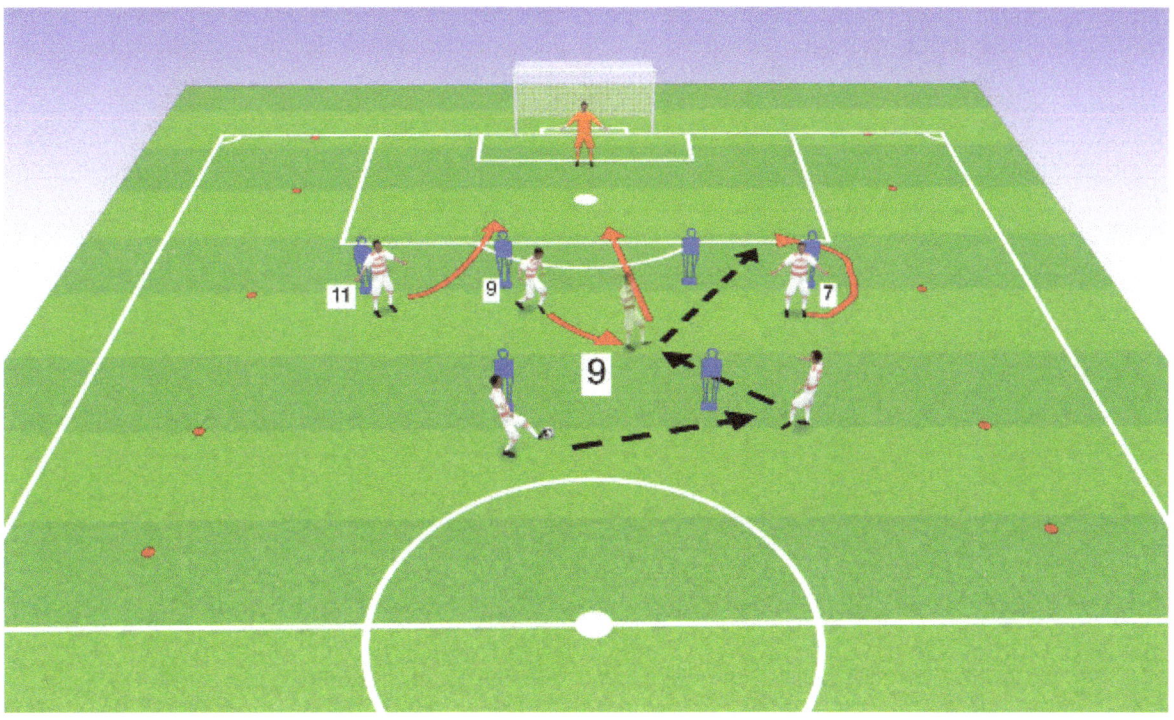

If 9 drops deeper, 7 and/or 11 can change the shape of their run and go down the outside of the full-back.

The pass now goes between the centre-back and the full-back mannequins.

Possible Progressions

Pass goes to 7/11 to feed 9 on a diagonal run.

Replace mannequins with defenders

- Start with just two centre-backs.
- Add a third defender.
- One midfield player can join in the attack for cut-backs from wider positions.

Chapter 10

Unit Work 3

Organisation

Place a line of cones approximately 30 yards from goal.

Team A's midfield players must stay behind the line.

Play starts with Team B's goalkeeper playing out from the back.

How to Play

Team B try to keep possession and work the ball into midfield.

Team A should try to press high and win the ball to create shooting opportunities.

Team A's midfield players can intercept passes into Team B's midfield and then join in attacks.

Possible Coaching Points

- Team A's forwards set traps to encourage Team B to play short.
- Aggressive press from the front three.
- Stop the forward pass – make play predictable – sprint to close down.
- Try to finish in one or two touches.

Developing Play in the Attacking Third (Finishing the Attack)

SSG

Organisation

Pitch is approximately 70 x 50 yards (the middle third is 20 x 50).

9v9 including goalkeepers.

Goalkeepers start the play but must play into their defensive third.

How to Play

Defenders can only play in their defensive thirds.

Midfield players can join in, in the attacking thirds.

One forward can drop into midfield to help the team in possession.

Possible Coaching Points

- Set traps when out of possession.
- Shape runs when closing down to make play predictable.
- Away from the ball, recognise cues and triggers.
- Press aggressively as a unit. (One sprints – all sprint.)
- Play quickly when counter-attacking.
- Look for runs/passes between defenders.
- **Quality of finish!**

11
Defending in the Defensive Third (Low Block)

> " I'm a defender, and my first job is to make the team secure at the back; that's my primary responsibility. "
>
> **César Azpilicueta**

Practice 1

Warm-Up Extension (15 mins)

Chapter 11

Organisation

Pitch used, as shown.

Box at the top of the 18-yard box is approximately 40 x 30.

How to Play

Both teams have a ball and start with the deepest player (a centre-back who then steps in to play).

Both teams pass the ball with realistic patterns and pace (move the ball quickly).

The final pass to the deepest player restarts the actions.

Defensive Principles (30 mins)

Organisation

Areas as previous practice.

All play starts with the deepest Team B player.

Use the 18-yard line as an offside line.

Defending in the Defensive Third (Low Block)

How to Play

Team B's objective is to score.

Team A defend the goal and can clear to a target player if they have space to do so.

The focus is on Team A, but Team B need to be managed: to make realistic combinations and to create scoring opportunities.

Possible Coaching Points

- Recognise key defensive points (18-yard line and 30 yards from goal).
- Stay compact.
- Communicate.
- Pass on runners (Don't follow).
- Squeeze forward a yard if you force play backwards.
- Open body position to keep track of attempted blind-side runs.

Defensive Principles 2 (30 mins)

Organisation

Remove the box and play in half a pitch.

Chapter 11

The target player from the previous practice becomes a crosser (either side, to simulate an overlapping full-back).

How to Play

Team B are encouraged to attack without using the crosser.

All play as before (match tempo, Team B use combinations to break lines, etc.).

If the attacks are stalled, the target player can be used to cross (maximum two-touch).

Possible Coaching Points

- Stay compact in front of the goal.
- Distance between players in the same unit, and from the back line to the midfield line, must be maintained.
- Defenders need to try to seize the initiative if the attacker has a poor touch.
- *Defenders must be prepared to block shots! Be brave, put your body on the line to protect the goal!*

Practice 2

2v2 (20 mins)

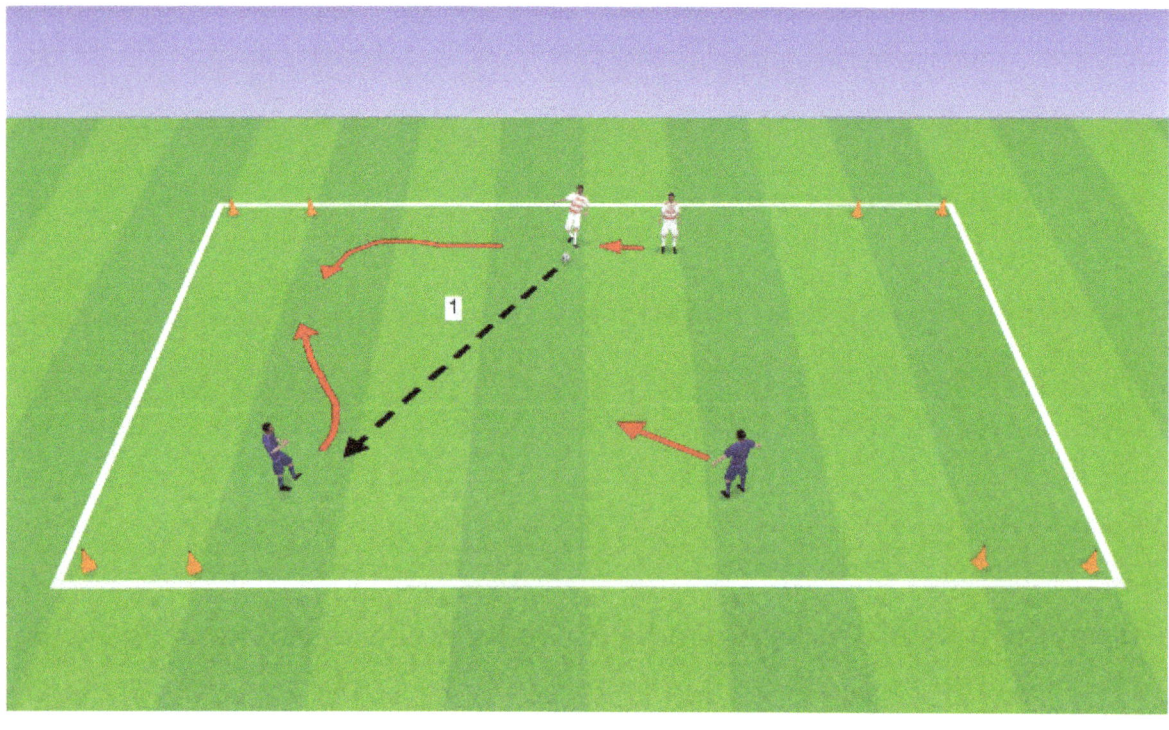

Defending in the Defensive Third (Low Block)

Organisation

The area is approximately 15 yards wide by 20 yards long.

Use large cones to make a small goal (one-yard wide) in each of the four corners of the area.

How to Play

Team B can attack either goal behind Team A.

Team A have to prevent Team B scoring by working as a pair.

Possible Coaching Points

- Communication.
- Close down quickly – they are close to your goal!
- Initial movement must take the defender between the ball and the goal to prevent Team B from scoring with one touch.
- Body shape – show inside or outside? Why?
- Second defender – cover position; close enough that if the first defender gets beaten, he is in a position to delay the attack.
- If Team B players cross over each other and switch sides – follow across centre line or pass on the ball carrier?

Chapter 11

Pressing and Transition (20 mins)

Organisation

An area large enough to accommodate your players but small enough to challenge them.

Divided, as shown, with a coned area in the middle for the defending team.

Three equal teams.

How to Play

Team C try to win the ball.

Team B must make five passes before they can pass to one of Team A.

When the ball is passed to a player from Team A, his teammates must sprint to his area, and a different Team C player tries to win the ball.

Team B will then disperse to the spare boxes.

Possible Coaching Points

- When in possession (not the session focus) – passing, receiving, and movement. Quick transitions.

Defending in the Defensive Third (Low Block)

- When out of possession (main focus) – angles of approach, speed of movement, use the lines as a defender to force the ball out of play, self-sacrifice!

Progressions

Reduce the number of passes required.

Add a second defender to win the ball back.

The defending team play to a target (goal or coach) on the outside if they win the ball cleanly.

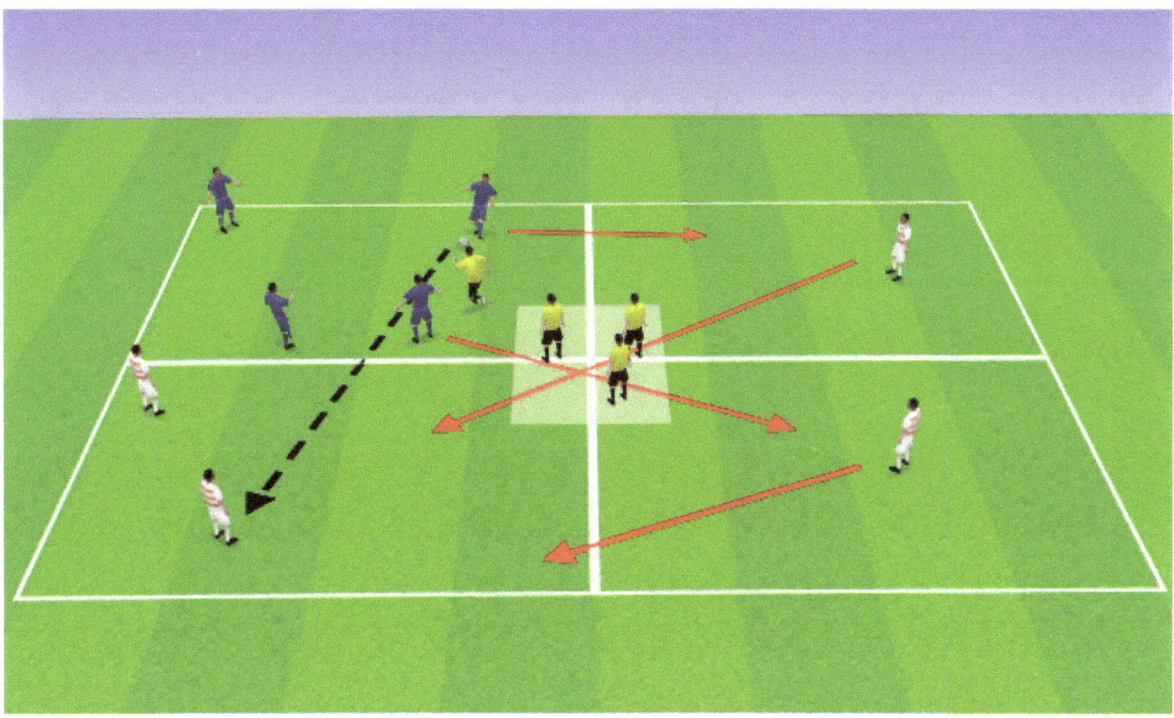

Movements

The lines show the movements that need to be made after the final pass has gone from Team B to Team A.

Hatched line denotes the pass; solid lines denote player movement.

Chapter 11

Defending in Final Third (40 mins)

Organisation

Set up the defence in the formation you expect to play.

Use flat discs to mark out key areas:

- Area 1 for blocking shots, aggressive press, tight marking, and emergency defending. (Bodies on the line!)
- Area 2, if the ball is in here, the opposite Area 2 (on the other flank) can be left free (midfield shuffle across).
- Area 3, midfield players to be compact, full-back must be narrow. (Surrender Area 2 on either side.)

Team A can play out from the back or play longer to a target player on halfway.

Defending in the Defensive Third (Low Block)

Practice 3

1v1

Organisation

Area approximately 30 x 30 (smaller for young players).

Work both sides.

A group of defenders (Team A).

A group of attackers (Team B).

A goalkeeper.

How to Play

Defender in a wide position plays a pass to the attacker at the top of the box.

He plays into another attacker on the edge of the area with his back to goal, who tries to score.

Rotate after each practice.

Chapter 11

Possible Coaching Points

- Defender should be able to see the pass coming into the attacker.
- Decision – intercept or hold up?
- Can you win it as he turns?
- Adjust feet quickly.
- Stay between the ball and the goal.
- Stay on your feet.

2v2

Organisation

Area as previous practice.

Players line up, as shown.

Rotate after each attempt.

Offsides in play.

How to Play

Wide attacker plays the ball to the support striker.

Defending in the Defensive Third (Low Block)

On the support striker's first touch, a defender sprints in to make a 2v2. (Adjust the start position of the defender, if necessary).

The supporting attacker plays forward to the striker and joins in to play to a finish.

Possible Coaching Points

- All those from previous practice.
- Communicate together.
- Show the attacker away from goal.
- React to deflections and blocks.

SSG

Organisation

The area is 44 x 50 yards.

Offsides from the 18-yard lines.

Six attackers (Team B) v Six Defenders (Team A).

How to Play

GK plays the ball into Team B, who can combine to score (create overloads, etc.).

Chapter 11

If attackers leave their zones, they are restricted to one-touch.

After each attack, restart from the opposite end.

Possible Coaching Points

- All previous points.
- Quick decision-making.
- Mark the player or mark the space?
- If Team A win the ball, play to their team-mates at the opposite end.

Practice 4

Defensive Heading (20 mins)

Organisation

Players a suitable distance apart, depending on age group.

The Team A player can either be removed, or made passive, to allow a degree of success for Player B.

Defending in the Defensive Third (Low Block)

How to Play

Server can throw or kick, and plays towards the Team A player.

Team B's defender should try to win the header and play back to the server.

If Player A wins the ball, try to take the ball through the gate on the end line, and Player B defends 1v1.

Possible Coaching Points

- Get into the line of flight.
- Watch the ball all the way onto the forehead.
- Keep your eyes open and mouth closed.
- Try to head through the bottom half of the ball to get height and distance.

Defending 1v1 and 2v2 (20 mins)

Organisation

Area is 36 x 44.

Rotate the players from previous practice in, and vice versa.

Chapter 11

How to Play

Defending 1v1 in a central area

Player B serves into Player A to attack the top goal.

Player B then closes down.

Play to a finish.

Restart from the opposite end.

Progression

Play 2v2.

Defending – Heading (25 mins)

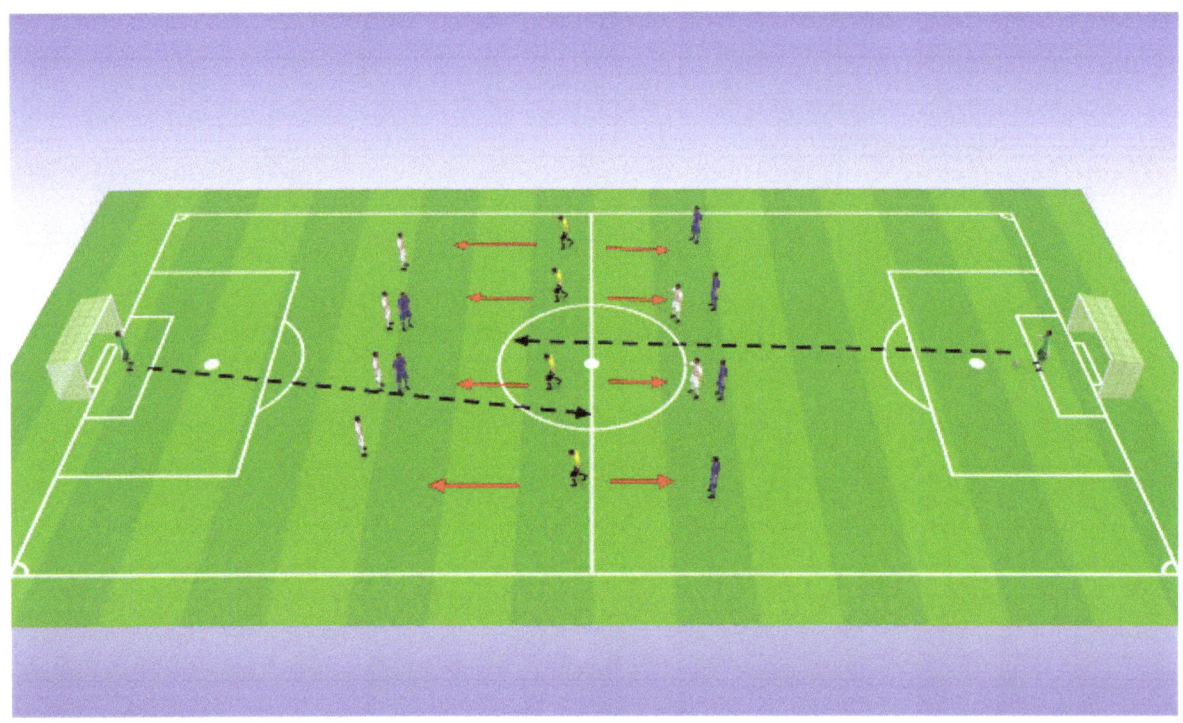

Organisation

Full-sized pitch

Defending in the Defensive Third (Low Block)

How to Play

Play starts from a goal kick and the defenders should try to head the ball into midfield. (Attackers can be semi-passive to start.)

When the midfield players (Team C) take possession, two of them join the attackers and play to a finish.

The midfield four attack both ways.

When the action is over, restart with a goal kick from the opposite end.

Possible Coaching Points

- Timing of the jump and header.
- Attacking the ball at the highest point.
- Defending as a unit whilst recovering towards their own goal.

SSG (20 mins)

Organisation

Pitch size to suit your players/numbers.

Equal numbers (if possible).

Chapter 11

How to Play

Normal rules with the following exception: if the goalkeeper makes a clean catch or receives a back pass, he MUST deliver into the opposite half.

12

Transitions from the Defending Third

> " In football, everything is complicated by
> the presence of the opposite team. "
>
> Jean-Paul Sartre

Practice 1

Pressing and Transition (30 mins)

Organisation

Area is approximately 35 x 25 yards.

Chapter 12

Split the outfield players into three teams, with two goalkeepers in mini-goals.

How to Play

Teams B and C combine to keep possession away from Team A.

Teams B and C score a point for every ten passes.

If Team A win the ball, they should try to score in either goal as quickly as possible.

Possible Coaching Points

- Defending team to press aggressively as a unit.
- Move as the ball moves.
- Try to make play predictable.
- Set traps.
- When you win the ball, try to score quickly.

Functional Practice (30 mins)

Organisation

The area is 40 yards wide by 30 yards deep.

A mini-goal is behind the defenders (Team A).

Transitions from the Defending Third

Three coned gates are behind the attackers (Team B).

The defending team should replicate your match team's playing style (so it could be a back three with two central defensive midfielders).

The offside rule is in play.

How to Play

Team B try to score in the mini-goal.

Team A should defend the goal and can score points by passing or carrying the ball through any of the gates.

Possible Coaching Points

- Hold the defensive line.
- Move together at all times (either up and down the pitch with the ball, or from side to side).
- Try to anticipate the next pass.
- Look for interceptions on weak passes.
- Secure the ball with the first touch.

Getting the shot away (pass) early.

Progression

Introduce a goalkeeper with a full-size goal.

Chapter 12

Functional Practice 2 (30 mins)

Organisation

Half a pitch with coned gates, as shown.

Teams as per the previous picture.

Offside rule is in play.

How to Play

Team B try to score in the goal.

Team A should defend the goal and can score points by passing or carrying the ball through any of the gates.

If Team A recover the ball in central areas, and can play to a full-back running beyond the outer gates, they are awarded two goals.

Possible Coaching Points

- As previously.
- Try to be progressive when the ball is recovered.

Transitions from the Defending Third

SSGs (20 mins)

SSGs to finish the session.

Two or three minute games with "bounce" players on the outside (on two-touches).

Different conditions, e.g., can't pass backwards, one-touch finish, one or three touches for the outfield players, etc.

These types of SSG are more of a fun way to finish off a session, but you can still reward the focus of the previous parts of the practice (e.g., a successful forward pass after a tackle in the defensive half can be worth a goal).

Chapter 12

Practice 2

Throw-Ins (30 mins)

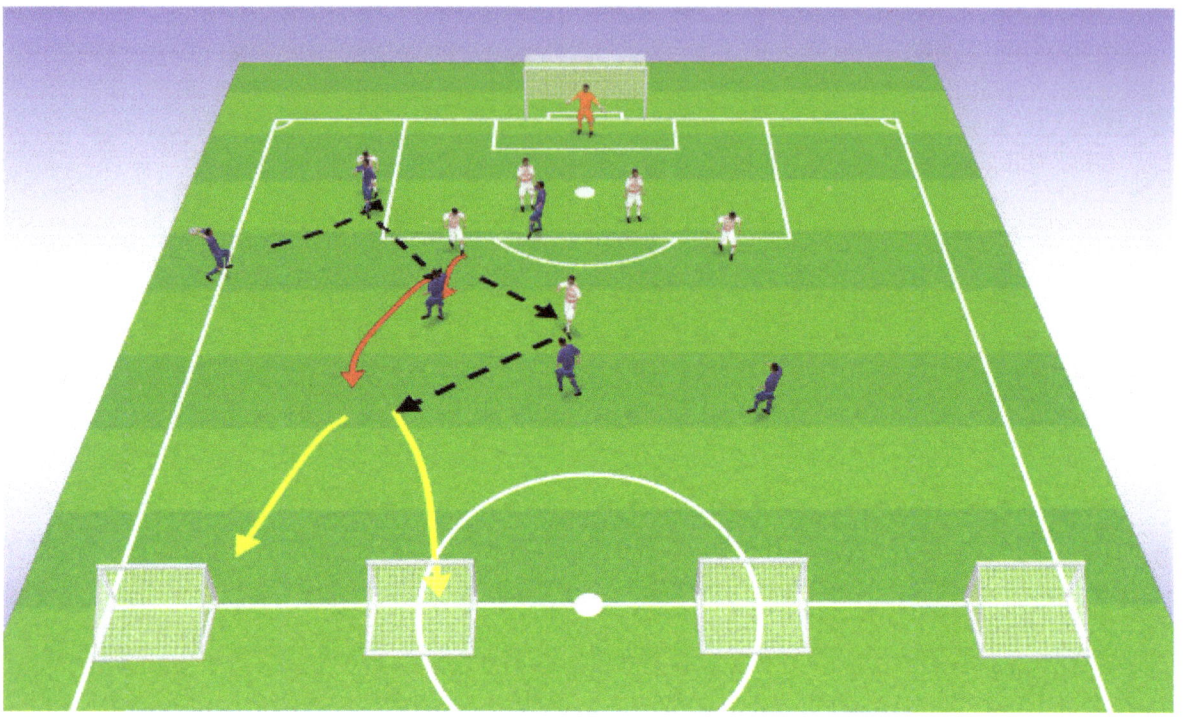

Organisation

Half a pitch with four mini-goals on the halfway line.

Team A have a goalkeeper, and six outfield players, in a 4-2 formation.

Team B has six players who can play anywhere.

How to Play

The first practice starts from a throw-in, and Team A must immediately press the ball.

If they win the ball, they must score in any of the mini-goals within six seconds.

Normal football rules apply.

Progressions

Use different restarts to develop the mentality to transition *immediately* on winning the ball, including free kicks.

Transitions from the Defending Third

Possible Coaching Points

- When out of possession – mark goal-side and ball-side of the attacker; appropriate distances between members of the same defensive unit; appropriate distances between defensive and midfield unit; communication.
- When in possession – secure the ball at the turnover; try to play forward quickly; pass forward; run forward; play into the goals with accuracy and pace on the ball.

Wide Free-Kick (30 mins)

Organisation

As per the previous practice.

How to Play

The practice starts from a wide free-kick, and Team A must defend the ball into the box.

If the goalkeeper can claim the ball, the full-backs should sprint forward and wide, whilst watching for the ball.

Centre-backs should split towards the corners of the 18-yard box.

Chapter 12

One of the central-midfield players should move towards the halfway line whilst the other shows for the ball.

The central-midfield players should be prepared to rotate positions in order to get free and play out from the back.

Try to score in any of the mini-goals within six seconds.

Normal football rules apply.

Progressions

Use different restarts to develop the mentality to transition immediately on winning the ball, including free kicks.

Possible Coaching Points

- As per the previous practice.

Central Free-Kick (30 mins)

Organisation

As per the previous practice.

Transitions from the Defending Third

How to Play

The practice starts from a central free-kick, and Team A must defend the ball into the box.

The GK should ensure that the defensive wall stays outside the 18-yard box.

The GK should try to claim high balls between his goal and the penalty spot.

The defensive line should hold their position until the kicker is about to strike the ball, then drop slightly deeper towards the penalty spot.

Midfield players should drop to provide a screen once they see that the ball is being played into the box.

As the ball is played towards the LCB, he drops initially, then comes forward to challenge for the ball.

The CMs should face the ball and try to recover second balls.

Player movements if Team A recover the ball are as per the previous practice.

Press any loose balls aggressively to deny Team B any easy possession.

Try to score in any of the mini-goals within six seconds.

Possible Coaching Points

- Good team discipline to hold the line.
- Good communication.
- Make sure that someone is covering behind the defender who is challenging in the air.

Chapter 12

Practice 3

Pressure and Cover (20 mins)

Organisation

Pitch is 30 x 35 yards, with a five-yard central zone.

Balls are located centrally, off to the side, with the Coach.

Three equal teams.

How to Play

The coach plays a ball into Team A who attempt to connect five passes – then they can transfer the ball across to Team C to score a point. The ball must stay below head height.

Team B defends with two players against Team A.

The three remaining defenders screen the central area and try to intercept passes.

Play 90 seconds then rotate the defending team.

Transitions from the Defending Third

Progression

On interception, the team that gives the ball away become the defenders.

If the ball goes out of play, the coach restarts by passing the ball into play.

Coaching Points

First Defender tactics

- Make a decision which way to show the attacker depending on where you have cover.
- Curved run to show attacker one way or the other.
- Close down space early and quickly.
- Sideways on body position.
- Good defensive stance.
- Stay on your feet.
- Watch the ball.
- Be aggressive – initiate contact.

Second Defender Tactics

- Communicate to the first defender where to show the attacker.
- Provide cover.
- Be close enough to the first defender to step in and engage attacker if the first defender gets beat.

Chapter 12

4 v 4 - 6 Goal Game: Cover and Balance (20 mins)

Organisation

Pitch is 30 x 35 yards, with three goals on each end line.

Balls located centrally, off to the side, with the Coach.

Two equal teams with no goalkeepers.

How to Play

Teams play 4 v 4 and attempt to score in one of their opponent's goals.

All restarts are from a ball played in by the coach.

Rotate players after each play.

If you don't have 16 players, the players who are behind the goals should just rotate into the practice.

Possible Coaching Points:

- Concentrate – immediate transition from defending to attacking.
- First and second defender tactics as per the previous practice.
- Try to see the back of the player's shirt who is in front of you.

Transitions from the Defending Third

Defending Team

- Secure the regained ball.
- Try to play forward early.
- Support the play with forward runs.

SSG - Defending as a Team (20 mins)

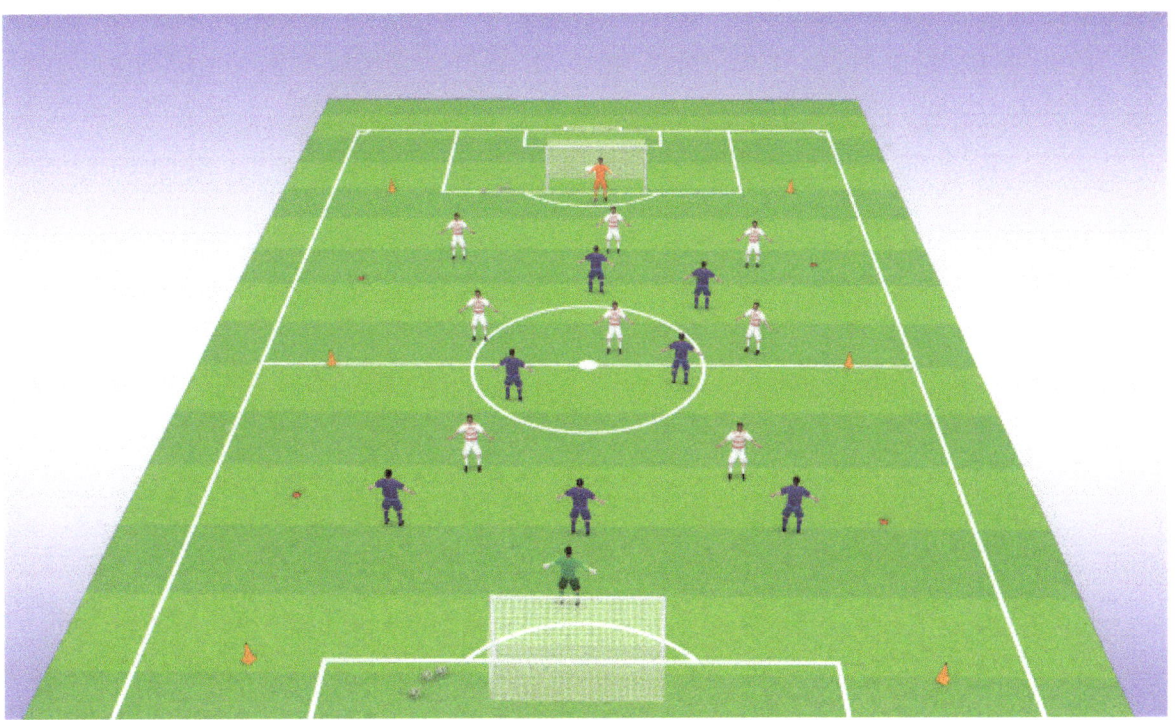

Organisation

The pitch should be a suitable size for your players, with a halfway line and goals at either end.

Two equal teams (if possible), with two GKs.

Balls distributed beside the goals to keep the game flowing when balls go out of play.

How to Play

Play a normal SSG with offside in play.

Restart from the GK when a goal is scored (the team that scores keeps possession) or when the ball goes out of play.

Chapter 12

Possible Coaching Points

- Reinforce all previous points.

Practice 4

Principles of GK Distribution

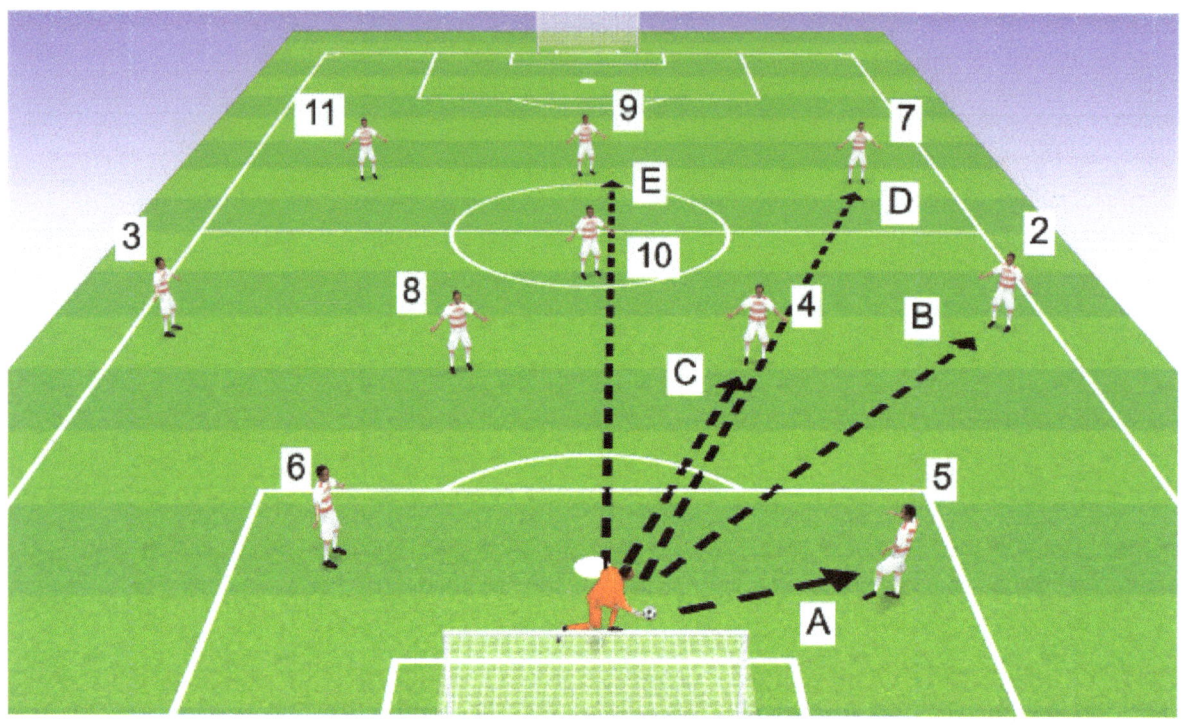

The following is just one of many ways to play out from the back.

In pure development terms, a short pass from the GK will allow for more development opportunities for all other aspects of the game.

However, the GK must make good decisions based on what he sees and in relation to how the opposition set up to defend against you.

Explanation

Players are numbered for a 4-3-3 formation.

Letters A to E are the options available (only the right side of the pitch for illustration purposes).

Pass A – roll out to the nearest defender if the opposition drop off to allow possession.

Transitions from the Defending Third

Pass B – kick or throw to the full-back who has advanced and moved as wide as possible.

Pass C – kick or roll to CDM, dropping short and at an angle.

Pass D – kick or throw to a wide attacker (practise overarm throws whilst running towards the 18-yard line).

Pass E – a viable option if your CF has been left 1v1, is quicker than his opponent, or where a quick counter-attacking situation can be exploited).

Distribution Game (20 mins)

Organisation

Full pitch. 11 v 6 (adjust numbers to your squad – this practice could be done as a functional practice by using your players from one half of the pitch, and coning off the other half).

How to Play

All play starts with a player from Team B playing long into the box for Team A's GK.

Chapter 12

Team B players can play anywhere and Team A should play, realistically, in their positions.

GK distributes to Team A, based on Team B's reaction to being out of possession (this can be dictated by the coach).

Team A play to the goal (15 seconds to score).

If Team B can recover the ball, they must attack as directly as possible. (Team A can be instructed to become semi-passive due to their numerical advantage.)

Possible Coaching Points

- Distribute accurately with kicks or throws.
- Try to leave the ball playable.
- Try to play to the correct side of the receiver (if he has space to run or play forward, make sure the ball goes in front of him).
- Try to play angled passes.
- Give good information with your passes. (Turn – hold – man on – etc.)

Scanning and Distribution (20 mins)

Transitions from the Defending Third

Organisation

Full pitch.

Equal teams with two goalkeepers.

GKs play in the centre circle (no one else is allowed in).

How to Play

Teams attack a nominated goal but can only score from inside the 18-yard box.

Any pass to a GK is also worth a goal.

GKs can receive in their hands, or to feet, and the GKs can challenge each other.

GKs can play to any of their team with kicks, throws, or rolls.

The GKs are permitted to try to score directly with a kick from their hands, but if they miss the goal, they have to run and retrieve the ball.

Possible Coaching Points

- All previous points.

NB. Whilst this practice is fairly unrealistic in terms of GK positioning, it allows plenty of opportunity to practice different types of distribution. From a Psychological and Social standpoint, it also moves the keepers from the edge to the centre of the practice.

Conclusion

I strongly believe that every training session there has ever been, has probably been delivered by now, but the way they are delivered – and the audience that they are delivered to – will constantly evolve. As a coach, you will need to know the level of detail that is appropriate to your players.

These sessions are designed around the 11-a-side game, but I believe that they can be delivered to 12-year-olds taking their first steps in the bigger game, as well as to adults. Some of these sessions have been adapted from sessions that I have observed delivered to players in the professional game, and then adjusted to fit the age groups of the players that I work with.

If used correctly, these sessions can give you a full season's work which covers every aspect of the game in every area of the pitch. Remember that, for players to fully grasp a concept, a degree of repetition may be required – you don't need to reinvent the wheel constantly! If a session works, repeat it again with your own subtle tweaks, and the players will begin to recognise these situations when they occur in games.

Whether you work with your players once a week or every day, having a logical syllabus to work from should ensure that you leave no area uncovered. This book gives you in possession, out of possession, and transition sessions which, along with a consolidation week (where you or your players decide what you are going to work on), provide a framework to build your season month-on-month to provide a full season's worth of sessions.

The numbers that I have used only serve as a guideline and, as every youth coach knows, planning has to be adjusted on-the-go if players don't turn up or additional ones that you weren't expecting do!

Rest assured that if you are reading this book, you are already making a massive contribution to young players' lives. Your players will look to you for guidance on their football journey, but you will almost certainly be teaching them life skills along the way.

Resilience, how to win and lose with dignity and humility, teamwork, friendship, and a passion for the game – among other things – are a by-product that should not be underestimated.

On a final note – a personal **thank you** for buying this book. You may not have known it at the time, but you are contributing to important research into a little known but horrible illness in Huntington's disease.

Just some of the other coaching books from Bennion Kearny

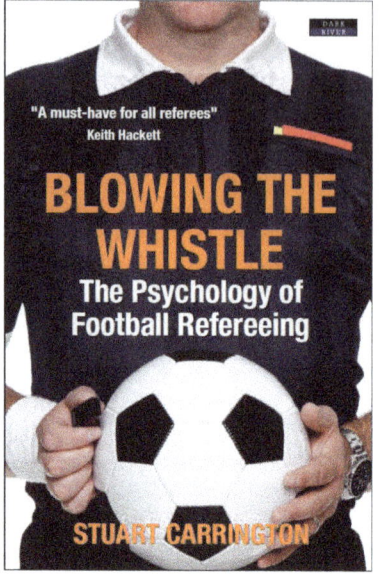

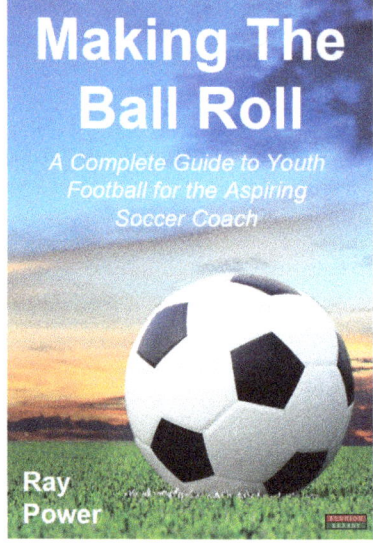
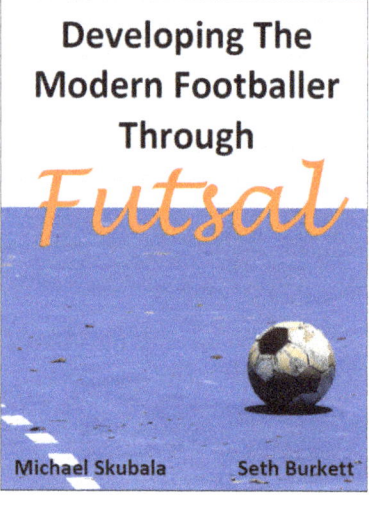

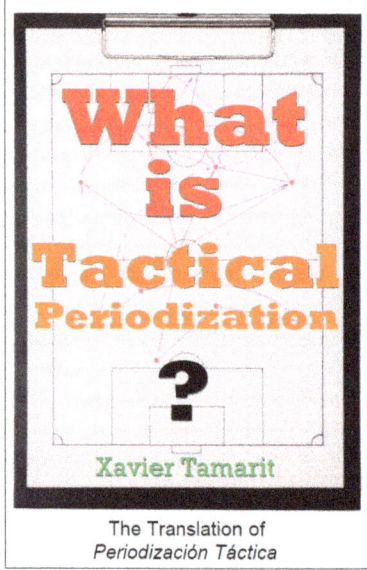
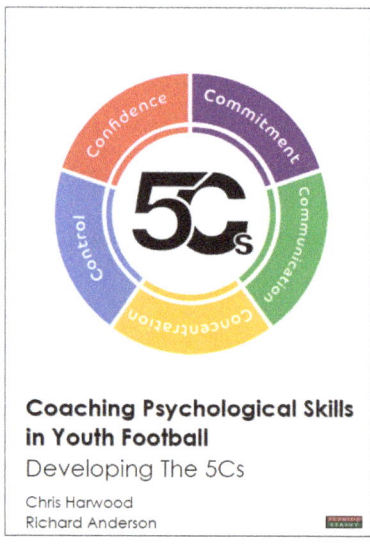

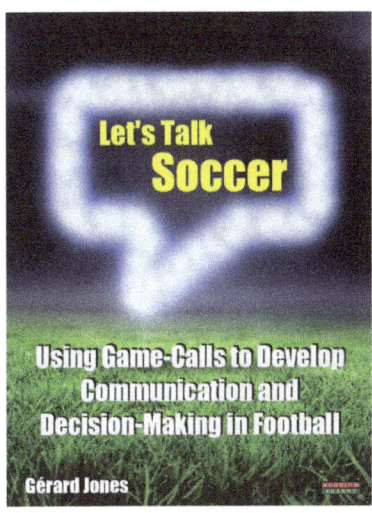

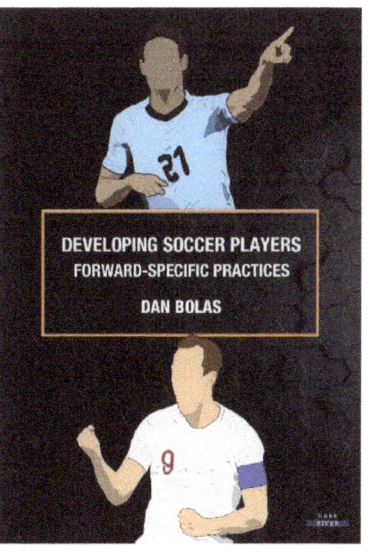

www.BennionKearny.com/football

www.ingramcontent.com/pod-product-compliance
Lightning Source LLC
Chambersburg PA
CBHW041131240426
43661CB00069B/2912